The Chartered Institute of Management Accountants

The Chartered Institute of Management Accountants

CIMA

Publishing

Environmental Management, Environmental Accounting and Financial Performance

J S Toms

(University of Nottingham)

This publication arises from the research project 'Finance Performance Differentials of "Ethically" Managed Companies' which was funded with a research grant from the CIMA Research Foundation. The award of a Research Foundation grant, and the publication of findings in this format, indicates that the recipient has successfully passed two separate peer review processes, which also involved practitioner assessors. The views expressed in this publication are the author's own, and do not necessarily represent those of CIMA.

Acknowledgements

We should like to thank the Research Foundation of the Chartered Institute of Management Accountants for supporting this project. We also wish to record our gratitude to the managers and directors who spared the time to participate in the fieldwork and who discussed their international transfer pricing policies in detail. The researchers are also indebted to Mrs Veda Smillie who painstakingly transformed numerous files and notes into a legible and articulate report.

First published in 2000 by:
The Chartered Institute of Management Accountants
63 Portland Place
London
W1N 4AB

ISBN 1 85971 348 3

Transferred to digital printing 2006

Contents

Executive Summary

The research project investigated differences in performance between companies that pursue environmentally friendly policies and those that do not. The survey was based on relative financial performance data for around 250 large public limited companies in 25 sectors over a seven-year period. It has also used content analysis of 695 company annual reports during that period and a questionnaire posted to 959 investment professionals.

In accounting terms, the results show that engagement in certain environmental management practices approximates to a difference of about 4.5 per cent return on capital in favour of those companies pursuing such policies. Similarly, those companies are perceived to be of lower risk and hence benefit from a lower cost of capital. In this case, the differential is approximately 1.5 per cent.

An important reason for these differentials is that managers of firms investing in good environmental management practice are creating significant intangible assets, particularly an improved reputation. In turn, these intangible resources are helping to drive competitive advantage. Although related to firm size, reputation depends on actual environmental policies rather than halo effects associated with, for example, financial strength. Reputation is also associated with the accountability structures typical of the diversely owned public company. Hence, stock market accountability is a vital driver of environmental management strategy in the professionally managed public limited company. High-profile, entrepreneurial companies with strong environmental reputations are atypical, even though their standards of environmental management and reporting may be exemplary.

The annual report is a crucial strategic tool for environmental management. More specifically, it is an important means of signalling managerial strategy. It is instrumental in accrediting investments made in environmental management systems and processes and hence in creating reputation and competitive advantage. Alternative strategies, such as the Kitemarking of environmental management systems and environmental auditing, have little additional impact on environmental reputation and have no effect when detailed disclosures are also made in the annual report. To be fully effective, these annual report disclosures should reflect the monitoring and implementation of environmental strategies. They should set quantifiable targets and ideally report performance against those targets. As a process of accountability, this is effective because companies less committed to environmental protection will not be able to imitate them other than through less convincing, more generalised disclosures. Quantified disclosures have become the norm in 'environmentally sensitive' industries, and there has been an improvement in the quality of environmental reporting in the early to mid-1990s. To a large extent, this represents a genuine commitment of managerial resources. It is likely that such practices will become commonplace in all industries if, as expected, the environment continues to rise up the political agenda.

These trends also reflect pressures from the investment community. Investment professionals are likely to value the extension of capital budgeting methods to environmental projects. They look to the annual report as the main source of information on environmental management strategy. Moreover, they prefer specific, verifiable and quantified information rather than generalised rhetoric. Again, in line with other findings in the research, they believe that good environmental management will reduce the perceived risk of a company.

The discussion in this book also suggests lines of further enquiry. As such, although it is hoped that the results here will be useful and interesting, the project represents a staging post on a longer road.

Preface

This book is concerned with management policy, environmental accounting and stock market information requirements. It therefore addresses some fundamental issues concerning corporate strategy and financial reporting. The first chapter incorporates a discussion of these issues in the context of the rising challenge to business practice imposed by concerns about the environment. The research begins with a survey of investment professionals' attitudes towards environmental accounting. In turn, this leads to an analysis and review of the main trends in environmental reporting by UK companies in recent years. The unique contribution of the research lies in its use of a large sample database to test the relationship between environmental management and financial performance. There has been much discussion of this issue, but relatively few studies based on large samples of data. The main reason is that there is no readily available index of corporate environmental performance that is both reliable and encompasses large numbers of firms. Here, a possible index is identified: the annual survey of 'Britain's Most Admired Companies' as published in *Management Today*. This research examines whether or not this index can be relied upon to measure actual environmental performance. Having established the reliability of the data, the survey then examines the extent to which environmental performance is associated with financial performance. An economic theoretical framework supported by statistical testing is necessary for these tasks, because a large amount of research has already been conducted using equivalent data sets for US corporations. It is not the objective of this book to describe the theoretical framework or statistical testing in detail. Interested readers are referred to the CIMA Research Report *Financial Performance Differentials in 'Ethically' Managed Companies* that contains a more detailed theoretical exposition and summaries of the statistical results. Meanwhile, abbreviated outlines of theoretical material and highlights of the statistical surveys are presented in the chapters below.

Various people have played an important part in the development and completion of this project. I should like to thank all those at CIMA who have guided and encouraged this research, in particular Bob Berry, Rebecca Burrows, Martin Houldin and Danka Starovic. I should also like to thank Mike Brown for allowing me to use the detailed returns from his own 'Most Admired Companies' surveys. Earlier versions of the material contained in this report have been presented at conferences and seminars, and I am grateful to the participants for their helpful comments. In particular, I should like to thank Rob Gray, Denis Patten and Bill Crampton. The research report has also benefited from the helpful comments of two anonymous referees. Above all, I thank my wife Liz for her support and helpful suggestions.

Abbreviations

BATNEEC	Best Available Technology Not Exceeding Excessive Cost (provision of the Environmental Protection Act (see below)
CEP	Council on Economic Priorities (USA)
CER	Corporate environmental responsibility
EPA	Environmental Protection Act 1990
ES	Environmentally sensitive
MAC	Most admired companies
PCB	Polychlorinated biphenyl
SEC	Securities Exchange Commission (USA)
SIC	Standard Industry Classification
UNEP	United Nations Environment Programme

1

Introduction and Research Method

This chapter introduces the research problem and defines key terms. Relevant literature is examined briefly and the research method is described. An outline of the remaining chapters is then provided.

1.1 The meaning and importance of environmental management and environmental accounting

The unsustainable consumption of the earth's resources may be *the* most important issue of the twenty-first century, not just in the political sphere but in the corporate domain as well. Participants in the latter, whether corporate managers or investment professionals, need to respond to the impact of environmental pressures on their activities. Hence, there is a growing interest in the techniques of environmental management. For larger companies at least, environmental management involves an organised response to the requirements of a broader group of stakeholders, including lobbying groups as well as customers and employees who tend to reflect wider pressures in society. Inside the organisation, environmental management requires technical and business processes designed to meet new specifications and associated systems of data-gathering.

These techniques will be driven in part by legislation, especially where the view prevails that profitable corporate activity arises from the exploitation of natural resources. On the other hand, competitive processes and the attainment of competitive advantage may promote better environmental management, especially if one accepts the view that limiting the consumption of resources can also create opportunities to increase profitability and wealth for some firms, if not for all. Much depends on how environmental policies are measured and communicated, and this is why the issue is also relevant to accounting and finance professionals.

Notwithstanding the apparent precision of many accounting techniques, in the field of environmental accounting traditional definitions of asset and liability and cost and revenue tend to break down. The legislative view of environmental management would suggest that expenditures on environmental systems and processes be treated as costs. Conversely, under the competitive advantage view, environmental management expenditure is clearly more in the nature of an investment. In part, these competing views are matters of economic or accounting theory. As such, they are beyond the scope of the current enquiry. However, they can also be reconciled by empirical research into the link between environmental strategies and competitive advantage, and that is the main focus of the current study.

1.2 Objectives of the study

The overall objective of this study is to examine the proposition that companies engaging in environmentally friendly policies are more profitable than those that do not follow such policies. It is conducted with reference to the corporate economy of the UK in the 1990s. The general objective has several more detailed components:

- What are the principal mechanisms available to management in communicating their strategies to stakeholder groups?
- Which of these methods do investment professionals favour?
- Which of these methods are most commonly adopted in financial and other reports?
- Which of these methods are the most effective?
- What are the most important recent trends in environmental financial reporting?
- How do corporate managers create reputation in the field of environmental management?
- To what extent is reputation in environmental responsibility associated with superior financial performance?

1.3 Conceptual framework: stakeholders, governance and the resource-based view of the firm

A conceptual framework links the remaining chapters and is illustrated in Figure 1.1. It relies on several assumptions. First, assume that competitive advantage is equated with superior financial performance. Assume also that the payback from investment in environmental management systems is to a considerable extent in the form of improved reputation. Finally, assume that pressures from lobby groups and regulators are transmitted via the stock market and can therefore affect value. It follows that, as the diagram suggests, there are several important linkages. Specifically, actual managerial environmental strategies must be disclosed: there is little point in excelling in this area if it is concealed from the outside world. The creation of environmental reputation follows from disclosure. Finally, competitive advantage is determined by improved reputation.

While it is not the purpose of this book to develop detailed new theories, it is none the less appropriate to briefly sketch those elements of theory that are important to the way the study has been conducted. According to one view, 'the ultimate test for the usefulness of social reporting information is its impact on decision-making' (Dierkes and Antal, 1985). This view could equally be applied to environmental reporting. Because this survey is concerned with the costs and benefits of environmental activities from an accountant's perspective, this decision-usefulness approach forms the underlying perspective of the current research. Gray et al. (1995) advocate an overarching political-economy-based framework for stakeholder and legitimacy theory. It is beyond the scope of the current research to give full definitions of these concepts. For further detail on stakeholder theory, see Donaldson and Preston (1995);

Figure 1.1 Environmental management and environmental accounting

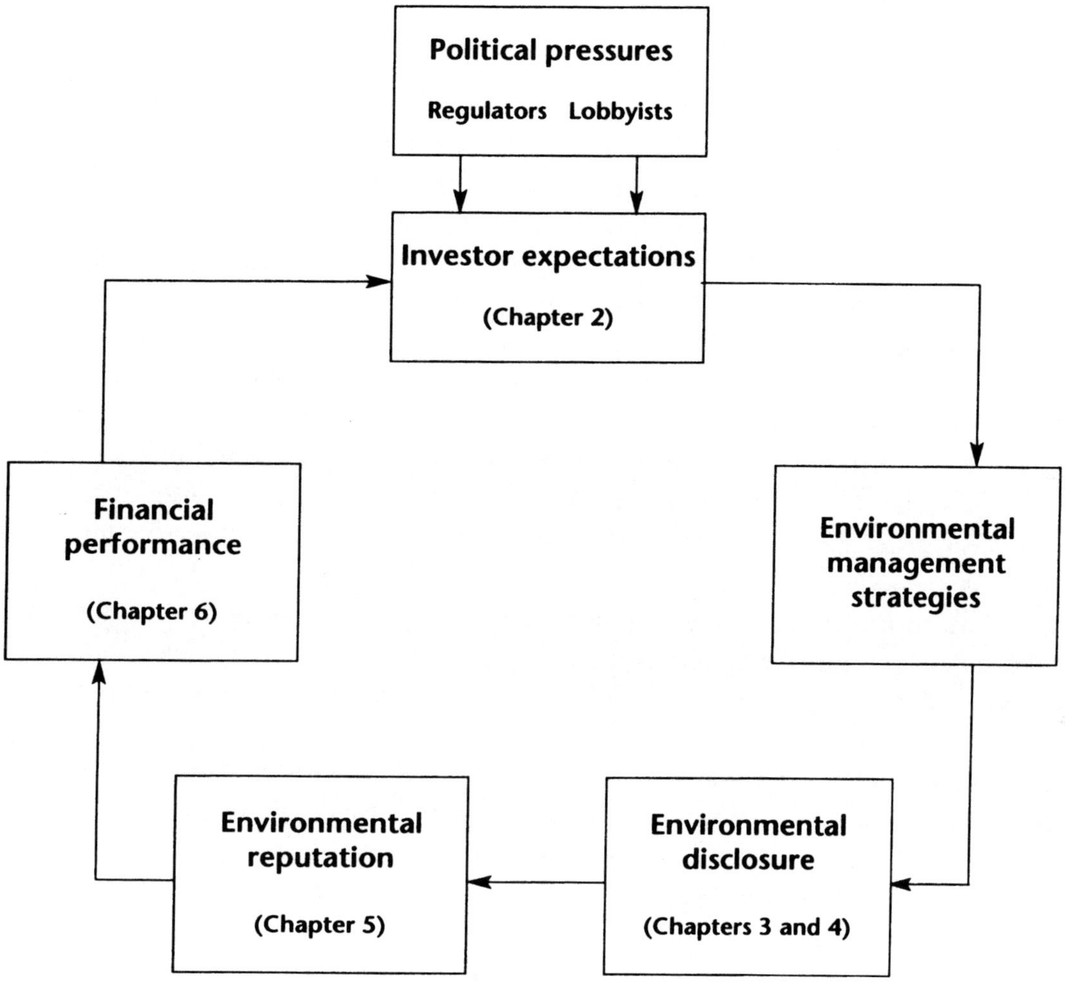

for legitimacy theory, see Patten (1992). The neo-classical view of political economy incorporates transaction and information cost, including those that might, for example, arise from the political process (Caporaso and Levine, 1992; Watts and Zimmerman, 1986). In the context of large, stock market traded public limited companies, such costs can be usefully termed proprietary and non-proprietary.

Proprietary information is defined as information whose disclosure changes the present value of the cash flows of the firm endowed with the information (Dye, 1986). The idea of proprietary information is useful as a potential explanation of investor decisions on the basis of rational response to managerial action. It also provides a theory as to why management should be concerned with stakeholders (such as the environment) other than the immediate shareholder group. Moreover, it provides a framework to model the actions of value-maximising management. On the surface, it might be expected that environmental disclosures are 'non-proprietary' (i.e. they have no effect on shareholder wealth). However, the Brent Spar incident provides a useful illustration of the relationship between external stakeholders, such as public pressure groups, regulators and quasi-governmental organisations, environmental lobbyists, and proprietary information. In such cases, the actions of lobbying groups unconnected with the firm can affect management environmental strategy, the company's reputation and possibly the stock market value of the firm (Zadek et al., 1997). A good example of the impact of such actions on share price was the Greenpeace demonstration against Rechem plc's shipment of PCBs into Liverpool. The refusal of the port authorities to allow the company to land the PCBs led to an immediate 10 per cent fall in share price (*Independent,* 12 August 1989). Share price declines are not always temporary reactions to news events. Exxon suffered a more prolonged period of underperformance compared with its competitors following the oil spill of 1989 (Cannon, 1994). More formally, in line with economic theory, it might be argued that there is a penalty for internalising costs that are usually external to the firm. In welfare economics, this is referred to as the 'Pigovian Penalty' of non-compliance (for example, see Heyes, 1998). As a result, management must recognise that external stakeholder groups can take actions that affect cash flows and shareholder value. One of the main purposes of this survey is to examine the relative importance to managers of the actions available to such groups, in particular pressure groups and regulators.

In formulating policy, there are two areas that management should consider. These are: (1) underlying environmental strategy, and (2) disclosure policy. Where underlying environmental strategy is a strength of the company, disclosure is important to draw attention to the fact. Where underlying environmental strategy is inadequate, disclosure can be used to obfuscate or draw attention away from the firm's weaknesses. Both are means whereby management may seek to *legitimate* the company's activities (Gray et al., 1995). For the investor, it is difficult to distinguish between these two motives without having access to the firm's decision-making process. Accordingly, an investor may perceive the risk (and therefore risk-adjusted expected return) to be similar across firms, whereas it is actually different. This may be because managers do not share certain information (adverse selection), or because some of their actions are unobservable (moral hazard). Under these conditions, according to the so-called 'signalling hypothesis', managers have an incentive to signal if there are higher returns to disclosing companies (Watts and Zimmerman, 1986). For certain environmental policies, where information asymmetries are high and management incentives to disclose truthful information are low, the crucial question then is, would the market believe false information and alter the value of the company?

An example of information asymmetry would be where management can invest in substandard equipment and cause pollution, including breaches of regulations, but where shareholders are unable to monitor the risk to which such policies expose them. Developments in the signalling hypothesis suggest that, where certain conditions are fulfilled, true signals will be believed and false ones rejected. These are that management must have appropriate incentive to disclose, the signal must be difficult to imitate (for example, by a competitor firm attempting to make the same claims), there must be an observable relationship and, finally, it must be cost-effective (Spence, 1973). These arguments are similar to those suggesting an incentive structure for firms to submit themselves voluntarily to external audit (Jensen and Meckling, 1976). For environmental disclosures, it follows that specified, quantifiable and verifiable information will be perceived to be of higher quality. A firm whose management is not actually pursuing environmentally responsible policies would find it more difficult to imitate a genuine competitor if that firm followed such a quality-signalling strategy. The obvious place for such signals is via the annual report. However, other signalling devices are available (for example, quality Kitemarks), as are other channels to transmit the signal (for example, press releases). There are thus many permutations of device and channel. The signalling hypothesis also depends on the relationship between managerial agents and investors. For example, larger, institutionally controlled firms might be expected to face greater scrutiny from analysts and fund managers than smaller firms. Lobbyists and regulators are also more likely to translate previously non-proprietary costs into proprietary costs for such firms. This would be more likely for firms in certain sectors and with certain product ranges. Where costs are proprietary, signalling should, in theory, be a strong predictor of managerial behaviour.

Consistent with quality signalling is the strategic management resource-based view of the firm. This explains competitive advantage in terms of inimitable qualities, for example those encapsulated in intangible assets. The resource-based view of the firm is exemplified in Porter (1985) and Barney (1991), and more recently applied specifically to environmental management (Porter and Van der Linde, 1996). Hall (1992) applies the resource-based view to intangible assets and reputation. At the same time, intangible assets are less easily perceived in financial markets, and therefore their management fits sensibly with a signalling framework. For the purposes of the discussion below, environmental management and the creation of environmental reputation are considered as instances of this view of intangible resources. However, in the present analysis, the resource-based view of the firm is extended to consider the owners of the business as a stakeholder group. Notwithstanding managerial resource endowment, pressure from shareholders may affect managerial capacity to develop new strategies. This may be a function of the manager–shareholder agency relationship (Jensen, 1986), or of managerial (in)ability to act as the strategic situation dictates (Barker and Duhaime, 1997). These issues have certain implications for the current research. However, the purpose of this research is to examine the relative effectiveness of quality signals, given that they are likely to reflect actual managerial strategies. Previous studies have not followed the signalling approach, which in the past has been applied to financial but not environmental disclosures.

Stock market value of the shareholder's investment is a conduit for the pressures of other stakeholder groups and for managerial quality-signalling of environmental strategies. Because the pressures from other groups are reflected in the value of the shareholder's investment, this relationship is referred to below as 'an extended single stakeholder model'. It follows that, in shareholder-value terms, the modern organisation, unlike its predecessors, cannot afford to ignore public pressure. Indeed, it might be argued that managers must go further and be proactive with the environmentalists and regulators (Guthrie and Parker, 1989; Roberts, 1992; Porter and Van der Linde, 1996).

Recent studies have attempted to develop theoretical frameworks for interpreting social (and hence environmental) disclosures. These can be broadly grouped into three areas: the stakeholder perspective (Ullmann, 1985; Roberts, 1992), legitimacy (Guthrie and Parker, 1989; Patten, 1991; Neu et al., 1998) and political economy (Tinker, 1991; Gray et al., 1995). The stakeholder approach in particular allows the simultaneous analysis of voluntary and regulatory pressures. In these studies, environmental disclosures form a subset of social disclosures, and that practice is also followed in the discussion that follows. The underlying framework used in this study synthesises the extended single stakeholder model with proprietary information cost- and quality-signalling (see also Figure 1.1).

When signals are transmitted via accounting reports about environmental performance, managers are usually attempting to communicate facts that will enhance the firm's reputation. However, reputation is difficult to quantify and standard accounting practices provide little guidance. Management accounting decision-makers need to know the payback of new capital investment, say in environmentally friendly technology, but reputation-based benefits will always be imprecise. As the above discussion suggests, however, reputation is becoming an important determinant of competitive advantage. Any research that can approximately quantify the payback from investment in reputation is therefore justified. Consequently, it is important to derive a quantitative measure for reputation. Like the large number of US studies that precede it, this survey uses a 'Most Admired Companies' (MAC) index of corporate environmental reputation. The British MAC surveys have produced a valuable and important data set reflecting peers' perceptions of reputation during the 1990s over a cross-section of British industry. At the time of writing, in contrast to the plethora of outputs based on the equivalent US data, no research using the UK data has yet been published. One particularly neglected area is the relationship between these measures of environmental reputation and financial performance. Results from US surveys in general show a positive relationship. However, this may to a certain extent reflect compliance with the stricter environmental regulations that prevail in the USA.

Where management attitudes towards the environment are arrived at in a more permissive climate, there are broadly three strategic alternatives. The first is the view that business is essentially a philanthropic activity. Traditionally, this has been reflected in the activities of a minority of the business community. Very early examples include the model industrial settlements at New Lanark and Saltaire. These were attempts by entrepreneurs to impose their own ethical standards on a wider community, a practice later emulated by companies such as Cadbury (Wagner, 1987; Bradley, 1987).

Philanthropy of this sort is the complete opposite of the second possible stance: the commonly assumed objective of profit maximisation. This might suggest, at first sight, that management should have no concern with corporate environmental responsibility (CER) where such activities incur cost on behalf of the shareholders (a more recently echoed and increasingly common version of this view comes from the shareholder-value-analysis school). The broad assumption is that all stakeholder groups benefit where management's objective is the maximisation of the investment value of a single stakeholder group, the shareholders (Friedman, 1962, 1970; Levitt, 1970; Moskowitz, 1972). For a discussion of the shareholder-value approach, see Copeland, Koller and Murrin (1994). Thus, as the agents of the shareholders, executives have no obligation to engage in socially responsible projects.

There are several objections to this view which form the basis of a third possible stance: the argument that expenditure on community and environmental projects is part of a conscious strategy of profit maximisation (Arlow and Gannon, 1982; Frederick et al., 1988). Thus, a profit-maximising firm could still recognise that expenditure on environmental projects, although involving short-run cost, could in the longer run constitute a saving, for example by anticipating the future impact of environmental legislation. Rather than cost, such expenditures might be said to constitute investment in goodwill-based assets. Friedman (1962) makes an exception for investment in 'goodwill'-type assets that might be expected to increase profits. Given the difficulty experienced by accountants in defining and measuring goodwill, the Friedman argument risks becoming a tautology. So, for a profit-maximiser, goodwill is defined as an investment that increases profits; investment that increases profits is defined as goodwill. For current purposes, it is appropriate to separate the profit-maximising duty/rational investor view from the goodwill/ethical investor perspective (for example, see Mahapatra, 1984). As discussed earlier, in the resource-based view of the firm, goodwill assets are regarded as determinants of competitive advantage.

Of the above alternatives, the first would be expected to occur in a minority of businesses regardless of the impact on profit. The second would, on the other hand, produce better returns for the ownership stakeholding group as a pay-off for avoidance of discretionary CER expenditure. Only the third would be consistent with an observed profit and investor return superiority to 'ethically' managed companies, or to what might be termed 'enlightened self-interest'. This view is consistent with the extended stakeholder model proposed above and suggested in Figure 1.1. As an extension to the resource-based model of the firm, this model suggests that pressures from regulators and lobbyists can be translated into proprietary costs for shareholders (assuming the extended stakeholder model). On the other hand, managers will attempt to avoid such costs by adopting higher-quality environmental management processes. Investment in such processes will create reputation-based assets, competitive advantage and superior financial performance. This hypothesis forms the underlying motivation for the research and is tested in detail in the ensuing chapters.

1.4 Overview of the project

On the basis of the conceptual framework discussed in the previous section and set out in Figure 1.1, the study goes on to examine five main areas. These are:

1. An investigation into investor perceptions of corporate environmental responsibility, conducted by means of a questionnaire circulated to fund managers and analysts (Chapter 2).

2. A descriptive analysis of recent trends in environmental disclosure. The analysis is based on a sample of 695 annual reports for large UK plcs in the period 1991–7 (Chapter 3).
3. An inferential statistical analysis of determinants of environmental disclosure. The analysis uses the same sample of annual reports (Chapter 4).
4. An inferential statistical analysis of the relationship between environmental disclosures and environmental reputation. The analysis is based on the sample of annual reports in Chapter 3 and the detailed responses for a similar number of companies to the annual survey of Britain's 'Most Admired Companies' (Chapter 5).
5. Environmental reputation and financial performance are compared, using for the above sample stock market and accounting variables (Chapter 6).

A final chapter (Chapter 7) presents some overall conclusions from the research. In all chapters statistical results are presented graphically. Detailed tables of data description and inferential statistical results are available in the CIMA Research Report, *Financial Performance Differentials in 'Ethically' Managed Companies*.

2

Investor Perceptions of Corporate Environmental Responsibility

This chapter is concerned with good, bad and indifferent managerial practices towards the environment and how such actions are interpreted by the investment community. These issues were investigated by means of a postal questionnaire. Results from the survey are discussed below.

2.1 Managerial strategy, environmental accounting and stock market response

There is a tendency for accounting and finance thinking in general, and management accounting in particular, to adopt the principles of shareholder-value maximisation. The link between action at the corporate level and stock market response is therefore especially important. In the case of environmental policy, the issue is more problematic since there may be a perceived conflict between the maximisation of shareholder value and the concerns of other, non-proprietary, stakeholding groups. A further problem arises from the usual association of environmental strategies with other aspects of social responsibility and ethics. Investment management is thereby made more complex. Only a relatively narrow definition of 'ethical' would prevent many large companies from being screened out of portfolios for one reason or another, and the broader the screening criteria, the greater the potential sacrifice in fund performance. For example, the most common screening devices used by ethical fund managers, such as exclusion of companies involved in arms, alcohol, tobacco and gambling, might exclude about 12 per cent of the FT All-Share Index from an ethical portfolio (*Bloomberg Money*, 'Ethical Investment Guide', July 1998). None the less, recent growth rates and investor returns in 'ethical' investment funds suggest that such conflicts may be more apparent than real. There are now 35 funds offering socially responsible portfolios to investors compared with eighteen in 1991, a growth rate of twice that of normal funds over an eight-year period. Ethical pensions alone have increased by about 28 per cent per annum, from £672m in 1994 to £1.4bn in 1997. In the USA, the increase has been even more dramatic, where ethical funds have grown from $12bn in 1995 to $96bn in 1998 (calculated from Perks et al., 1992; 'Green Pensions Bloom', *The Times*, 18 October 1997; and *Bloomberg Money*, 'Ethical Investment Guide', July 1998).

So, given the increased profile of 'ethical' investment in the fund management industry over recent years, what exactly are analysts and fund managers looking for when selecting shares to meet ethical investment criteria? Relatively little research has been conducted into how they actually interpret signals about corporate social and environmental responsibility and place value on managerial action. Furthermore, within those studies, few separate the environment from more general ethical issues. This survey, by contrast, is concerned exclusively with the environment.

The approach followed in developing the questionnaire is based on the research method outlined in Chapter 1. Accordingly, particular emphasis is placed on signalling, effective or otherwise, as a device for communicating good environmental practice to the markets and the consequences of such signals for shareholder value. Previous empirical surveys were reviewed, and their results used to inform the current approach where applicable.

An important aspect of investor demand for CER information is its perceived importance relative to conventional financial measures. Previous studies have examined this issue. Most of these have ranked CER in terms of perceived importance against lists of other types of accounting data, usually well down long lists of rankings including mainly financial variables (for example, Belkaoui, 1984; Benjamin and Stanga, 1977; Chenall and Juchau, 1977; and Firth, 1979, 1984). The consensus from these surveys is that CER is considered to be of 'moderate importance' (Gray et al., 1995). However, all these studies pre-date the rising trend of environmental disclosure from 1987 also evident from the research of Gray et al. (1995). In the light of this pattern of research, an objective of the present study is to quantify the relative importance of the environment to the investment community.

Previous empirical surveys have tended to identify a common set of contingent factors that might lead to greater environmental disclosure. Most common among these are factors such as size, sector and profitability (for example, Cowen et al., 1987; Trotman and Bradley, 1981). It follows that these criteria might also be important in the research activities of analysts and the selection criteria of fund managers.

2.2 Survey design

To investigate the issues discussed in the previous section a questionnaire-based method was adopted. There were two reasons for this. First, while interviews might have been preferable on some grounds, it is typically difficult to gain ready access to investment professionals. Second, previous published surveys have used questionnaires, and therefore it is appropriate here if results are to be compared. It was not intended to replicate any previous survey exactly, partly because the population has changed through time, and also because the purpose of the questionnaire was to establish hypotheses for further testing in subsequent parts of this research. Accordingly, a five-module questionnaire was developed, with each module relating to one of the objectives of the survey. Each questionnaire was colour-coded and was accompanied by a covering letter explaining how each respondent was selected, indicating support of the sponsoring organisation, with an assurance of confidentiality and a reply-paid envelope. The questionnaires were deliberately limited to two sides of A4 paper in length.

The objectives were to establish the relative importance of the components of managerial strategies on, first, environmental policy, and second, on disclosure of those activities. In doing so, it was considered important also to identify contingencies beyond the realm of short-term managerial decision-making. For example, firm size, ownership structure, sector, etc., might be expected to have some influence. These objectives are similar to those used in previous studies (Rockness and Williams, 1988; Harte et al., 1991). A further objective was to compare the attitudes of fund managers and analysts drawn from funds with ethical investment criteria and those concerned only with traditional indicators. Such a split was justified by empirical findings from earlier surveys (Gray et al., 1995), the theoretical reasons for a trend towards fuller disclosure outlined above, and the *a priori* expectation of differing information needs of these two groups (Harte et al., 1991). However, if the trend towards fuller disclosure can thereby be extrapolated into the future, the criteria currently being used by ethical and green funds will become important for all funds. To summarise, the objectives of the study were as follows:

- To assess the relative importance of corporate environmental performance to the investment community.
- To identify the contingent circumstances that influence managerial CER.
- To assess the relative importance of various managerial policies in establishing CER with the investment community.
- To assess the relative importance of the method of disclosure of managerial policies in establishing CER with the investment community.
- To assess the relative importance of non-annual report-based publicity in establishing CER with the investment community.

A further objective was to compare the relative importance of these areas and the relative attitudes of subgroups within the sample, and in particular to compare the attitudes of ethical fund managers with those of other fund managers and analysts.

Responses were invited to a series of closed questions broadly grouped under the above five headings. The underlying distribution of responses was based on a Likert scale, tick-box grid where 5 = very important/strongly agree to 1 = not important/strongly disagree. A 'not relevant' box was also added where appropriate. A final box was added to allow respondents to make written comments.

The population was drawn from the listings of ethical and other funds in *Bloomberg Money* (July 1998) and corresponding individual contact names obtained from various Web sites and directories. This created a sample of 484 fund managers, of whom 28 were with ethical funds with an environmental investment policy. The remainder had no stated policy. A modified version of the questionnaire was also sent to analysts. A particular objective of this part of the research was to investigate how the analysts circulated in *Management Today*'s 'Most Admired Companies' survey arrive at their quantitative ratings for CER. This was important, given the reliance placed on these ratings in later stages of the research. Consequently, the sampling method was the same as that used in the *Management Today* survey, although it was not possible to obtain the same sample of named individuals. Within this constraint, the method was replicated as far as possible by selecting the same fund management companies and addressing the envelopes to the same groups of analysts. This produced a further subsample of 475 analysts in 25 investment organisations across 19 stock market sectors. The combined sample of fund managers and analysts was 959.

The overall response rate (57 out of 959, or 5.94 per cent) was relatively low. For the specifically targeted environmental fund managers, the response rate was much better (11 out of 28, or 39 per cent). A response rate of 39 per cent is typical of other recent questionnaire-based surveys of fund managers and analysts: for example, Yap, 1997 (39 per cent), Jones et al., 1995 (42 per cent), Firth, 1984 (38 per cent), Benjamin and Stanga, 1977 (35 per cent), and Chenall and Juchau, 1977 (46 per cent). Therefore, for the non-ethical investment professionals, it is very likely that the perceived irrelevance of environmental issues reduced the response rate to a large part of the investment community. Within this subgroup, the results are also probably biased towards responses from those regarding the environment as important, and lack of responses from those who regard it as an irrelevance. A positive consequence was that there were also a very small number of missing variables and very sparing use of the 'not relevant' boxes. Responses from the analysts by sector were as follows: capital goods, 1; chemicals, 2; food producers, 1; media, 1; mining, 1; oils, 4; stores, 1; support services, 1; transport, 2; utilities, 3; building and construction, 2. In two cases, the sector could not be identified from the returned questionnaire. Analysis of non-responses showed, unsurprisingly, that the response rate among 'ethical' fund managers was rather higher than the general average. Therefore, it might be expected that the mean response scores examined below are biased upwards, while the differences between the ethical and residual subgroups are understated. Given the small population of ethical funds, the sample size here is similar when compared with studies that have concentrated exclusively on ethical funds. For example, Harte et al., (1991) examined eleven ethical trusts via a questionnaire survey, and Perks et al. (1992) examined fourteen ethical trusts via a review of published investment policies. As long as investment professionals regard the environment as a peripheral issue, surveys will inevitably be based on small samples of niche funds. On the other hand, if environmental concerns in the political sphere increase pressure on the corporate sector the views analysed below will become increasingly representative of the wider investment community.

2.3 Analysis of responses

In this section, the questionnaire responses are examined under several headings: the effects of contingencies, management policies, accounting-based disclosure, and other, non-accounting-based publicity. The attitudes of 'ethical' and 'non-ethical' fund managers and analysts are also considered. Where appropriate, comment is included on the differing views of analysts and fund managers and of those based in ethical funds and those not.

2.3.1 Relative importance of the environment

Respondents were asked two questions about the relative importance of the environment. First, they were asked to indicate the importance of environmental criteria relative to financial performance measures. Second, they were asked to consider the importance of evaluating environmental expenditure relative to other types of capital investment. In general, and in line with previous surveys (Gray et al., 1995), fund managers and analysts regarded environmental responsibility relative to financial performance as 'fairly important' ('fairly important' = 34 per cent, with 9 per cent responding 'very important'), although a small majority consider it to be neutral or unimportant (Figure 2.1).

Figure 2.1 Importance of CER relative to financial performance

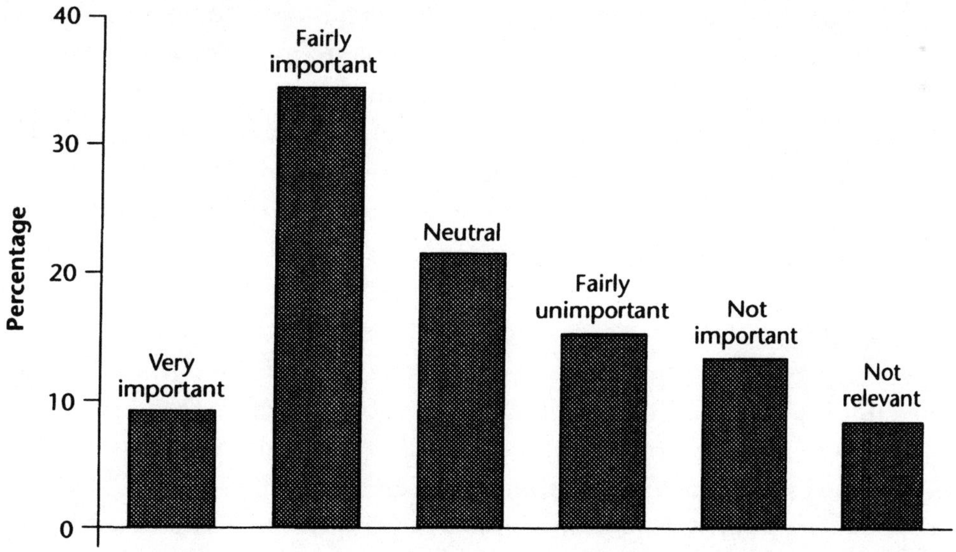

Use of the 'fairly important' box might reflect the twin hurdle approach adopted by some environmental funds. As one respondent to the survey pointed out, companies must be expected to outperform *and* satisfy the environmental stock selection criteria. A further statistical analysis showed that there was little significant variation in response within the fund manager and analyst subgroups.

The perception of importance increased when respondents were asked about the appraisal of environmental expenditure (Figure 2.2). There was a strong consensus that such cash flows are an 'investment' and should be appraised accordingly (72 per cent considered such appraisals to be important or very important), rather than be treated as an expense.

Figure 2.2 Importance of appraisal of environmental expenditure

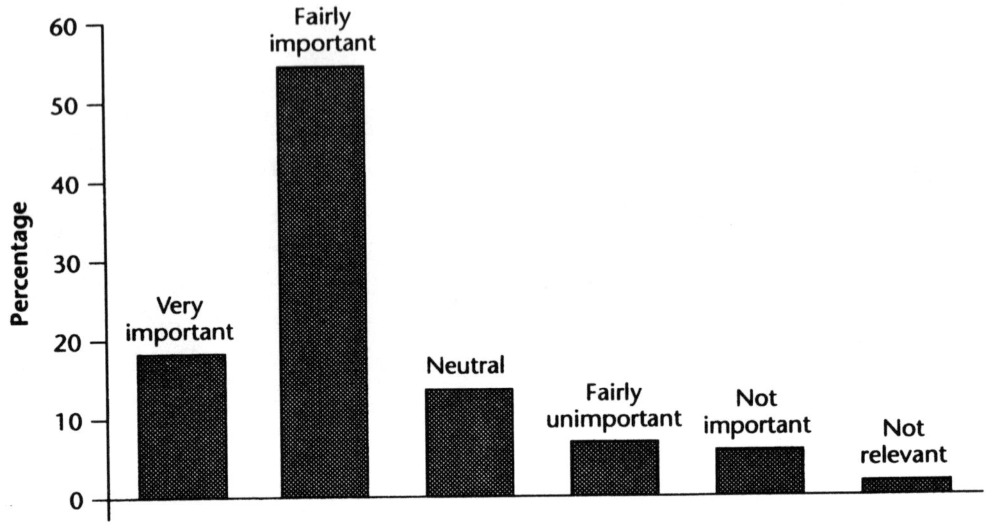

One respondent felt that corporate restructuring played a particularly important role in raising the profile of environmental expenditure and was 'good news for the environment'. The respondent used the example of a buy-out, a situation that 'normally involves environmental due diligence, and the development, if necessary, of an expenditure programme to make good any defects'. It is interesting to note that environmental expenditure was perceived to be important when specified as an investment project, but declined in significance when environmental responsibility was set in the context of ordinary financial return. A possible interpretation of these results is that the Environmental Protection Act (EPA), the 'polluter pays' principle, and the BATNEEC (Best Available Technology Not Entailing Excessive Cost) rule has impacted on the capital expenditure decision more than on the bottom line in general. (For a full discussion of these legislative provisions, see Howes et al., 1997, Chapter 6.) If so, the effect of the regulations has been to highlight the environmental consequences of capital budgeting within the investment community.

Another important comparison was to assess the relative importance of return and risk. In general, the responses indicated that good environmental performance is more likely to reduce risk to an investor than increase investor return (Figures 2.3 and 2.4).

Figure 2.3 Higher CER will lead to higher financial returns

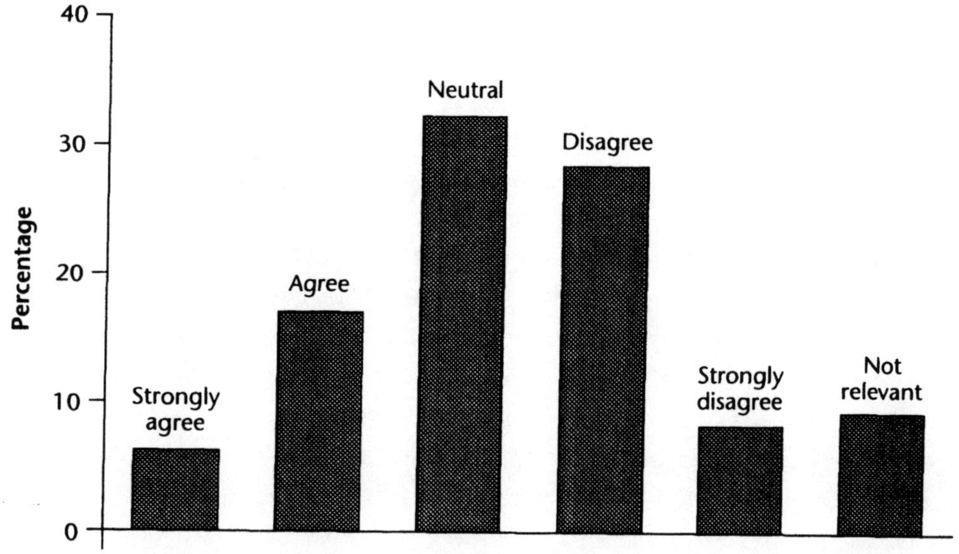

Figure 2.4 Higher CER will lead to lower risk

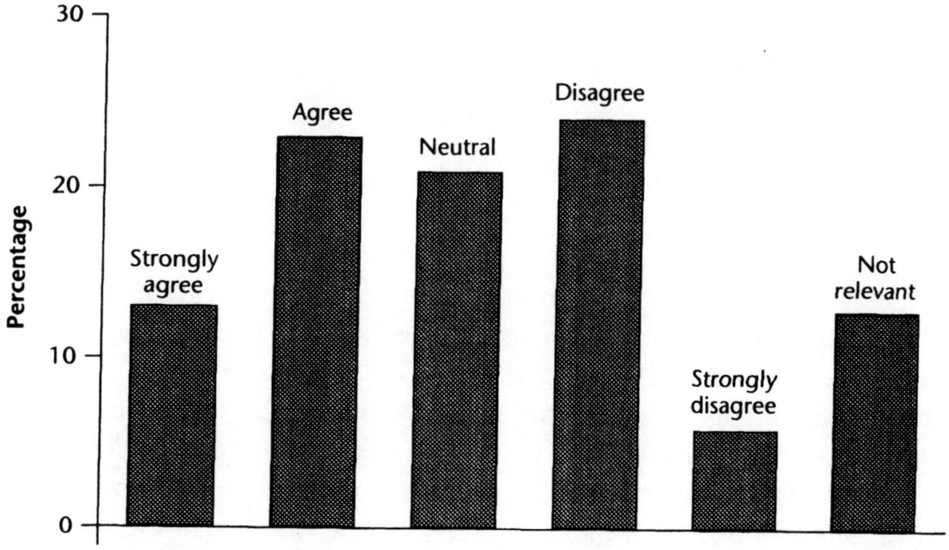

The mean importance score across the whole sample was 2.5965 for return and 2.807 for risk, although the difference at the aggregate level was not statistically significant. Within the sample groups, however, there were interesting contrasts. In particular, the analyst group, when compared with fund managers, considered environmental responsibility to be an important determinant of both higher risk and higher return. On the former count, the difference was highly significant. Conversely, when the attitudes of ethical and non-ethical fund managers were compared, there were no significant differences. Investment objectives, in terms of the apparent ethicality of the fund, do not appear to inform the expected financial outcomes of fund managers. This may indicate that, although it is impossible to select stocks from the full market portfolio when managing an ethical (or environmental) fund, managers appreciate that this is in any case a very difficult task. In other words, selection from an environmental universe of securities still allows sufficient diversification to obtain average market risk and return.

From the much higher scores of the analyst responses, it might therefore be inferred that attitude to the environment is governed by position in the organisational hierarchy. Fund managers are under pressure from legal constraints (for example, the outcome of the case of *Cowan* v. *Scargill* and other institutional restrictions, Perks et al., 1992), or may face risk-averse incentive structures to offer greater diversification. By contrast, analysts are sector specialists whose specialisation may encourage a more researched and detailed understanding of the risk–return trade-off. Furthermore, analysts are junior to fund managers in the organisational hierarchy: consequently, a further possibility is that age and career factors may influence their more bullish attitude to the possibilities of environmentally determined investment strategies. One analyst responding to the survey commented, with some lamentation, 'Emphasis on environmental policy is still, sadly, largely in the domain of "ethical" funds ... and perhaps does not yet enjoy the status it should.' Such a view might suggest that the environment could become more important in the future through promotion. However, this question was beyond the scope of the current survey when designed, and it is only possible to speculate at this stage. It is, none the less, an issue that would benefit from further research.

2.3.2 Contingency factors

Interpreting the above results, it is recognised that attitude towards the environment may be contingent on its perceived relevance as an issue. In turn, this may reflect various situational determinants of corporate environmental responsibility. Each contingency was based around a hypothesis derived from prior research. Those considered were first, size, and second, family ownership. The signalling hypothesis would suggest that both these factors would lead to lower environmental responsibility in the eyes of market participants. This is because smaller firms attract less scrutiny and family firms are less dependent on capital markets for financial resources. Both, therefore, have less incentive to engage in quality signalling about their managerial activities. Such a hypothesis presupposes that capital markets place a value on the environmental aspects of those managerial activities. On the other hand, it might be argued that smaller companies are more environmentally responsible. They face less capital market scrutiny in general and are more likely to be selected by managers of niche ethical funds seeking to avoid investments in larger firms involved in controversial activities (e.g. arms, alcohol, tobacco, etc.). Further, management may have greater freedom to concentrate on wider stakeholder issues and less on the bottom line. Similarly, there is the possibility that family-controlled firms might be more likely to engage in philanthropic activities of all kinds, including environmental projects.

The third contingency identified was prior profitability, on the basis that the managers of profitable companies have more access to free cash flow to fund environmental projects. Fourthly, sector specificity was considered, given that many previous studies have identified relationships between the environmental sensitivity of the sector and managerial responses. Lastly, linked to the sector and the nature of the corporation's activities, the product range was considered.

Figure 2.5 Determinants of environmental responsibility

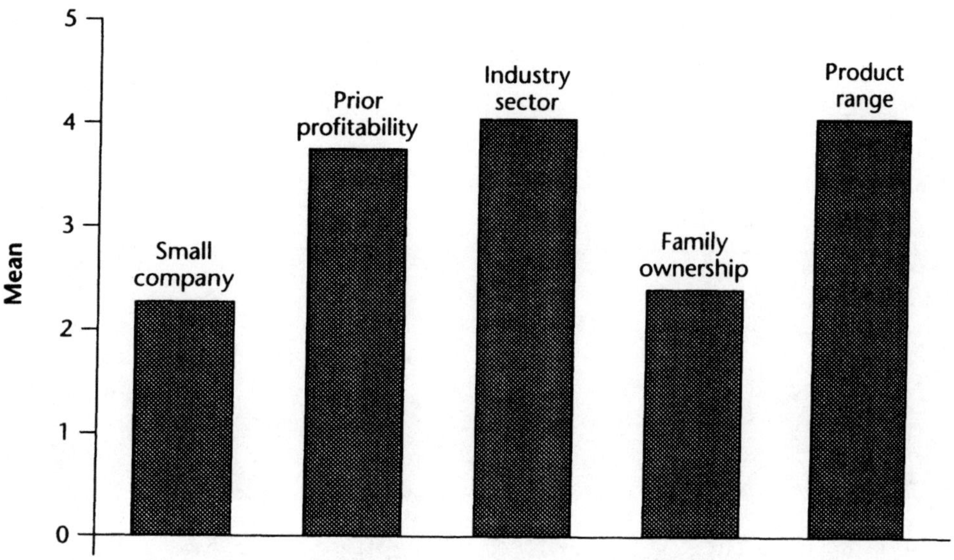

Figure 2.5 shows the relative importance of situational or contingent factors. For the sample as a whole, product range was the most important factor. Where product range was potentially damaging to the environment, investment professionals felt that greater environmental expenditure might be justified. The residual group of analysts and fund managers held this belief more strongly than the ethical fund managers, although the difference was not statistically significant. There was a similar pattern for sector specificity as a determinant of the level of environmental expenditure. Here, the overall mean was only slightly lower than the product range result, and again, the residual group scored higher than the ethical fund managers (although the difference was not statistically significant).

Prior profitability was the only other variable that a majority of respondents considered to be above average importance. There was a marginally significant difference between the ethical and residual subgroups, with the latter considering this to be a more important determinant of environmental responsibility. On ownership, there was consensus within all subgroups. Turning to company size, although it was generally believed that larger companies are more environmentally friendly, this view was less strongly held by the more ethical investor. Notwithstanding this observation, all respondents considered small companies and family-owned companies less likely to be environmentally responsible. The mean scores on these items (2.2807 for small companies and 2.3860 for family control) were not just lower than the others in the contingency section, but were lower than any other response score in the whole questionnaire. These results tend therefore to support the signalling hypothesis. Market participants perhaps feel that firms more readily subject to their scrutiny are more likely to behave in what they regard as a responsible manner. In conclusion, environmentally responsible firms are likely to be large, already profitable, and non-family controlled (for any given sector and product range).

2.3.3 Management policy towards the environment

This section addresses specific management policies towards the environment and how members of the investment community perceive them. Figure 2.6 illustrates the relative importance of management policies in creating an impression of environmental responsibility.

Figure 2.6 Important elements of management strategy in achieving environmental responsibility

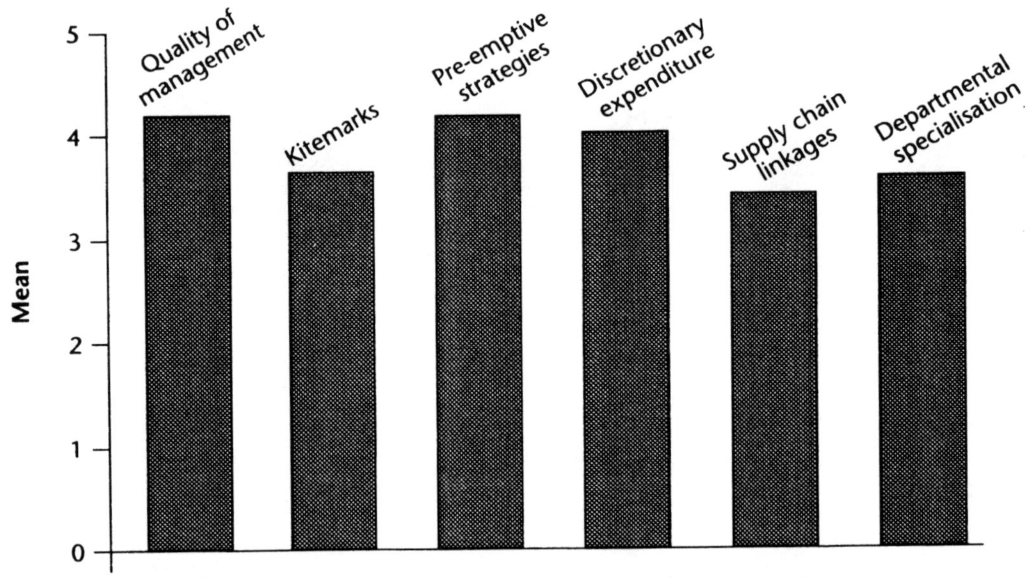

Environmental responsibility is more likely to be exercised where general management is already of high quality. This suggests that environmental management is not a distinctive set of attributes when compared with other managerial decision variables. Of the specific managerial policies set out in the questionnaire, pre-emptive action towards the threat of regulation obtained the highest average score. This may be taken as an indication that the market is likely to reward companies with first-mover advantages, including where those advantages are established in the environmental arena. One way to obtain them would be to engage in 'discretionary' environmental expenditure beyond the level required by current legislation. It would suggest that money spent on environmental protection might be interpreted generously by the market, especially, as noted above, where environmental expenditure is properly appraised.

Ethical fund managers were particularly concerned about monitoring the polluting aspects of company activities. The mean response was significantly higher for the ethical fund manager subgroup and was the most important consideration when compared with other managerial actions. Another factor, connections with environmentally unsound companies via the supply chain, also produced a marginally significant difference between ethical fund managers and the residual group. Again, while the concern of ethical managers about pollution and connections with polluting activities is high, such concern is not fully reflected in the wider investment community.

Kitemark awards, for example ISO 14001, had a relatively low average score (3.5263 for the full sample). Ethical fund managers considered them to be more important than other fund managers, but only at a marginal level of significance. On the basis of this evidence, it is possible that capital market participants are not overly concerned with Kitemarks. Alternatively, it may be that they are not believed to be a credible indicator of quality management. For example, ISO 14001 has been labelled as a 'missed opportunity' (Krut and Gleckman, 1998). These authors consider the standard to be 'falsely hyped' (Adams, 1998) and concerned only with management systems without linking them to actual environmental performance. Similarly, specialisation within firms via the creation of a separate environment department achieved only a relatively low rating across all subsample groups. Managerial action, then, as suggested by the importance of pre-emptive policies, appears more important than standard systems and processes, and management can score higher with the investment community where they are seen to be taking action to deal with anticipated outcomes.

2.3.4 Disclosure strategy

This section addresses the qualitative factors influencing the market's interpretation of corporate environmental disclosures. Figure 2.7 gives a clear indication as to how quality environmental information might meet the information requirements of the investment community.

Figure 2.7 Disclosure strategy and environmental reputation

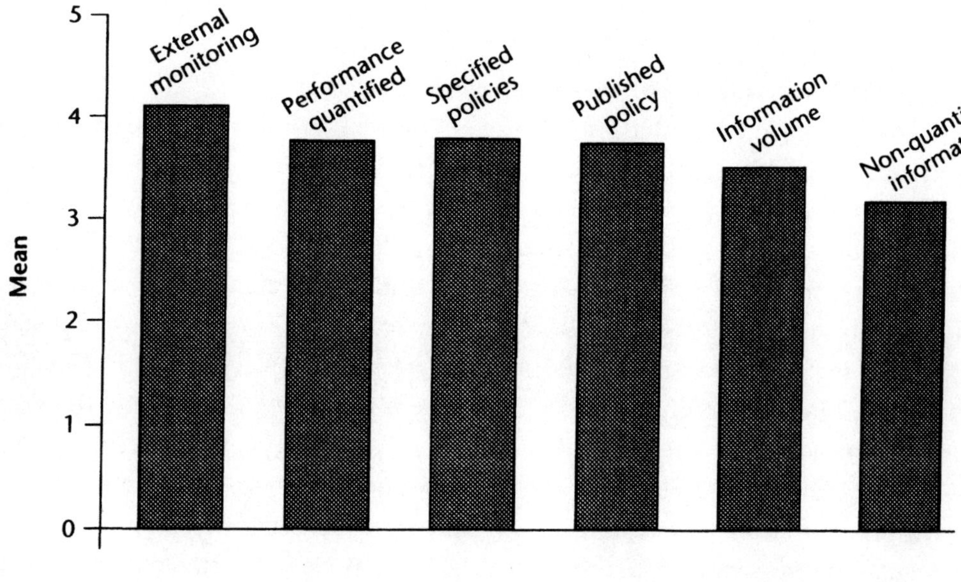

There are several important points to note. The first is that non-quantified information has a relatively low value. This is true for all investors, whether based in ethical funds or not. Non-quantification scored significantly worse than all other disclosure strategies to which responses were invited. The second point to note is the impact of the volume of information provided. Quantity of information is obviously appreciated and detail always useful, and this appears to add value to environmental disclosures where non-quantified data is used. Mere volume of information does, however, miss certain other valuable characteristics, in particular the extent of specification and the use of external monitoring. Again, ethical fund managers favour greater volume and may therefore be a source of pressure to expand the coverage of annual reports. The third point, related to the first two, is the extent to which policies are specified. Specification of policies was significantly more important than non-quantified data. It was also more important than a general statement of policy, although not significantly so. Managers of ethical funds find the act of specification significantly more important than other managers and analysts. The fourth point is that quantification is preferred. Lastly, the use of external monitoring appears to sit at the top of a hierarchy of disclosure strategies. This category of disclosure had a significantly higher average score than all the others. In addition, the ethical group thought it significantly more important than those based with ordinary funds. In all cases, the ethical group had higher mean scores for all categories of disclosure reported in Figure 2.7 (although not in all cases significant). Such a pattern suggests that the ethical investment community favours higher disclosure and, it follows, has an interest in promoting such disclosures through its investing activities.

To summarise, quantification is better than non-quantification; specification is better than volume of data, and external verification adds credibility to any data, however disclosed. A good reason, in line with the signalling hypothesis discussed in Chapter 1, is that quantified information is more readily verifiable. Consequently, the signal is of good quality since those firms not actually engaged in good environmental practice cannot follow suit.

2.3.5 Publicity and environmental reputation

Previous sections have examined the role of the annual report as a tool of corporate communication. In addition, other channels for communicating both positive and negative environmental information were examined. Figure 2.8 summarises the responses to survey questions on various aspects. On the left are aspects of publicity that management would normally seek to avoid, and on the right are mechanisms for communicating positive images of corporate environmental policy. On the negative side, the adverse publicity associated with fines is potentially very damaging to corporate environmental reputation. Fines produced the highest average score *vis-à-vis* other categories of response for the full sample group, with a very small mean difference between the subsamples. Accordingly, it is possible that the effect on reputation will be disproportionate to monetary cost. It is also likely that such effects will be more important in regulated industries, although such a relationship is not testable directly at this stage of the research. In contrast, charitable activities appear to offer little net benefit in terms of reputation building. Charitable contributions obtained a low average score for the full sample, although such actions seem to carry more favour with ethical fund managers. The evidence suggests that the reputation improvement per £ of charitable donation is less than the per £ loss arising from fines. Other evidence supports the view that avoiding the negative aspects of publicity is more important than developing the positive aspects. Negative press publicity was significantly more important than positive publicity as a determinant of environmental reputation. As one analyst commented when responding to the survey, 'environmental issues are of little or no relevance unless a company incurs a financial penalty or the risk of a financial penalty in the future'. On the positive side, tailored presentations and briefings to investor representatives are more effective than general press releases or charitable initiatives. Further, as the mean differences indicate, negative attention from pressure groups becomes more serious if it translates into negative press publicity. To summarise, outside environmental lobby groups and publicity are 'hygiene' factors. In other words, corporate managers should view the public relations function as a damage-limitation exercise and expect relatively poor returns from positive actions. The results here provide an interesting contrast to the generally positive interpretation placed on aspects of accounting reports as discussed above and reported in Figure 2.7.

Figure 2.8 Publicity and environmental reputation

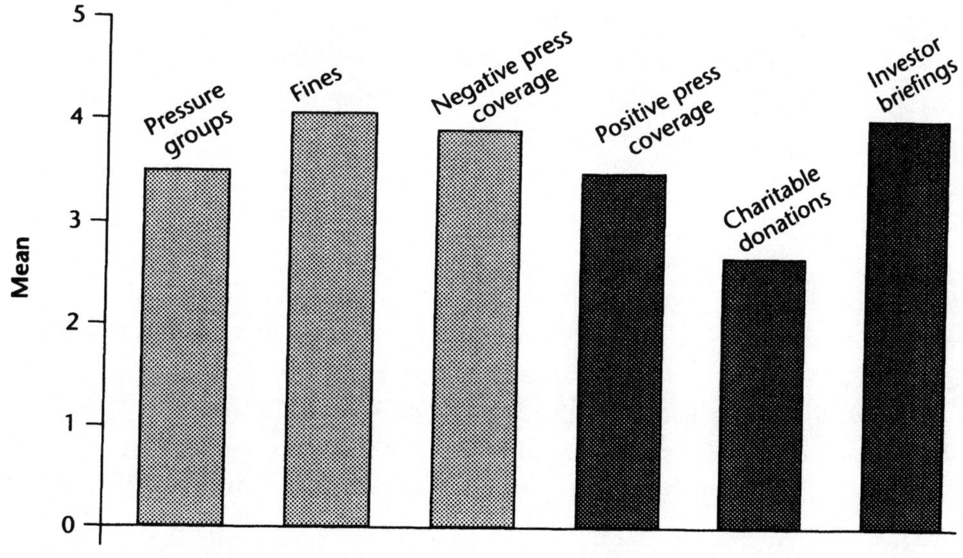

2.4 Conclusions

There were various limitations associated with the research. In particular, there are some disadvantages associated with the use of questionnaires. These are compensated in relation to, say, interviews, where a relatively large cross-section of observations can be obtained. In the current study, the sample size obtained was larger than in some previous studies but not large enough to avoid certain caveats. In particular, subgroups within the total sample were quite small (especially the ethical fund managers) and results should accordingly be treated with caution. Further research of this kind should either await a larger population of ethical fund managers or the end of apathy among other investment professionals. It is likely that these will come about simultaneously in the future. Until they do, the present study provides a pointer to the trends that might emerge.

Bearing these limitations in mind, the above discussion has compared the relative importance of environmental issues and management environmental strategies in five main areas. The first of these, the importance of environmental performance criteria against conventional financial ones, suggested two significant findings. These were that the extension of accepted capital budgeting techniques to environmental expenditure is likely to be well received by the investment community. It was also observed that, particularly among the analyst subgroup, good environmental management is likely to reduce the perceived risk of the company. As a second area, the survey then examined the influence of contingencies on perceptions of environmental management. The conclusion here was that the company's activities, as measured by sector and product range, were more important than prior profitability. It was also noted that larger, non-family-controlled businesses were more likely to be perceived as environmentally responsible. Thirdly, a series of management policies towards the environment were assessed. Here, pre-emptive strategies towards future legislation appear to be particularly important in establishing a reputation for environmental responsibility with capital market participants. Fourthly, the method of disclosure of environmental activities was investigated. There is a hierarchy of disclosure strategies, each step of which is more convincing to the capital markets. Thus quantification is better than non-quantification, specification is better than volume of data, and external verification adds credibility to any data, however disclosed. Lastly, aspects of lobbying and non-accounting-based publicity were examined. Channels of communicating positive news outside the annual report performed badly, suggesting that the annual report is an essential tool for managers in communicating environmental strategies to the capital markets. In addition, investor briefings may be a useful mechanism for communicating information about the environment.

The key point is that companies that follow the environmental policies listed below are likely to enjoy better reputations for environmental responsibility in investment institutions. To secure this reputation, management should consider the following:

- Engage in environmental expenditure beyond the requirements of current legislation and in anticipation of future legislation.
- Ensure that such expenditure is properly appraised.
- Make effective use of the annual report to add credibility to environmental management strategies. Publish quantified, auditable targets where possible and use them as benchmarks for actual performance.
- Support the annual report themes with presentations to investors.

3

Emerging Accountability? Environmental Disclosure Practices by UK Companies

This chapter examines trends in environmental reporting by UK companies. Previous research into UK disclosure practice has tended to rely on the measure by volume of content. This survey also used content analysis but, instead of counting words, measured the qualitative level of accountability represented by the disclosures. An index of disclosure quality was derived from the responses of investment professionals about the important attributes of environmental disclosure discussed in the previous chapter. The survey method was designed to accommodate a descriptive study of recent trends in UK corporate disclosure. A sample of 695 companies across 25 of the main sectors of the UK economy was employed. The study was especially concerned with environmental disclosure in the period 1993–7, and in particular to see if there was any underlying increase in the degree of accountability.

3.1 Environmental disclosure in UK annual reports, 1975–95

Despite a promising trend following the publication of the Corporate Report in 1975, during the 1980s only a small minority of UK plcs made any disclosure in annual reports about their environmental policies and performance. One survey found that, for a sample of the 50 largest companies in the UK, only 14 per cent disclosed environmental information, in contrast to 53 per cent in the USA and 21 per cent in Australia. Even fewer companies were disclosing specific information – for example, energy consumption. Another wide-ranging survey has also shown a similar pattern for the UK in the 1980s (Guthrie and Parker, 1990; Gray et al., 1995).

However, by the early 1990s new practices began to emerge. There were several aspects to this. The first was a rising trend in the number of companies disclosing environmental information. One survey of 108 finance directors selected randomly from the *Times 1000* found that 29 per cent had included environmental information in their annual report in the past, and that 39 per cent intended to do so in the future. Recognising that the situation was still changing, a further survey (Macve and Carey, 1992) concluded that it had become normal for the very largest companies to provide at least some information on environmental issues.

A second important trend was changes in the character of environmental reporting. In the annual reports of many companies, the level of environmental reporting in the 1980s was of such a low level as to be virtually meaningless. Companies employing higher standards of disclosure, meanwhile, had begun to make more specific statements, in particular to set out objectives and statements of policy (Tonkin and Skerratt, 1991; Harte and Owen, 1991, 1992).

Previous surveys have relied merely on volume measures of disclosure. For example, Cowen et al. (1987) used total number of disclosures for any particular category of social disclosure, including environment, by reference to the mean number of pages devoted to the subject for US data. Gray et al. (1995) use a similar method for British data. However, as one researcher (Wiseman, 1982) concluded, completeness and length are not representative of actual environmental performance, and in any case the voluntary nature of these disclosures undermines their credibility. Other US surveys have examined differences in qualitative levels of disclosure, for example by using the Council on Economic Priorities (CEP) ratings system (Roberts, 1992). For the UK, there is no such comparable rating system. None the less, partly because the quantification of disclosure is important for the tests discussed in subsequent chapters, a ranking system was required by the present study to quantify the degree of disclosure.

3.2 Survey design

The study uses data from annual reports to classify the general pattern of disclosure in the UK in the period 1993–7. The sample used was based on the companies covered by the *Management Today* 'Britain's Most Admired Companies' surveys. Most recently published annual reports for all companies appearing in the surveys for 1996 and 1997 were obtained. In addition, for the years 1993, 1994 and 1995, annual reports were obtained for one in two of those appearing in the *Management Today* sample. In some cases, at the time of data collection, the most recent annual report was for a year ending in 1996, in other cases for 1997. Where a report was initially obtained for a 1996 year end, the 1997 report was also obtained for that company if it became available during the data collection period. For years where sampling was used, firms were selected to maintain coverage across the 25 industry sectors featured in the *Management Today* survey. The total sample of annual reports obtained was 695 company/years (detailed breakdowns of the sample are given in subsequent tables). For the purposes of this and additional tests the variables examined are (1) the level and extent of disclosure, (2) the use of Kitemark accreditation, (3) the use of environmental reports, and (4) internal and external environmental auditing. The survey is not intended to be comprehensive. Rather, it is sample based and deals with trends affecting only those companies within the sample. In doing so, it seeks to inform subsequent tests based on the same sample. As a by-product it speaks to the general discussion about emerging trends in environmental reporting. The main disclosure variable used in this survey is a qualitative ranking system. At the theoretical level, such a hierarchy follows from the quality signalling framework proposed in Chapter 1. From the questionnaire of investment professionals in Chapter 2, it is apparent that a hierarchy of disclosure exists (Figure 2.7). As demonstrated there, for each qualitative improvement in disclosure, credibility is increased and the gap between actual managerial action and that indicated by accounting disclosure is reduced. Other authorities suggest that such a hierarchy may be consistent with good practice. According to the guidelines published by the United Nations Environment Programme (UNEP, 1994) a hierarchy of disclosure within an environmental report should consist of three levels. These comprise a category (a general issue of concern to stakeholders), an aspect (a specific issue about which information is to be reported), and an indicator (a quantitative measure of performance during a reporting period). The latter might include tonnes of emissions, water consumption per unit, etc.

For the purposes of further empirical investigation, the hierarchy suggested by the questionnaire responses in Chapter 2 was assigned a ranking score. This is shown in Table 3.1. Attempts to assess quality *a priori* suggest only an approximate rating system. The method used here thus had strong parallels with the approach used by Zadek et al. (1997). A similar approach to quantify levels of environmental and other ethical acts by corporate management was used in a prior study conducted in the USA (Robertson and Nicholson, 1996). This survey used a three-point scale of 'general rhetoric', 'specific endeavour', and 'implementation and monitoring'. As the research on UK companies progressed, it became apparent that the latter two categories tended to blur some important distinctions. For example, a company might state that it has an environmental policy (specific endeavour), but without stating the policy itself. Similarly, at the implementation and monitoring level, some companies published targets, but only a few would go so far as to report actual performance against target. The content analysis was therefore performed according to the rating system shown in Table 3.1. The ratings were applied by a second researcher, independently of the main researcher and without knowledge of the general objectives of the research. A subsample of scores was cross-checked against the scores allocated by a third independent researcher. Finally, the principal researcher checked a sample of scores. Throughout, only a small number of discrepancies were observed (less than 5 per cent). These procedures ensured that the ratings were accurately, consistently and objectively applied.

For each company for each year, an environmental responsibility score (ERS) was assigned accordingly. This provides a qualitative measure of disclosure. From the findings in Chapter 2, higher-rated companies indicate quality in the sense that expectations of a section of the investment community are being met. In using this method it was also possible to monitor the total proportions of companies making any disclosure at all. It is therefore feasible to continue some of the studies referred to earlier by monitoring the overall trend in disclosure throughout the 1990s.

It was also considered useful in this part of the survey to consider general trends associated with other aspects of environmental management. Data was therefore collected for the full sample on the disclosure of Kitemark awards (KITES), the use and reporting of internal (INT) and external (EXT) environmental audit (EA), and the publication of a separate environmental report (ER). From the questionnaire survey of investment professionals (Chapter 2), these were felt to be of some importance, although KITES were rated lower than the EA and ER. This raised the issue of whether the main KITES for environmental management systems, BS7750 and subsequently ISO14001, had been a failure. A possible reason for perceived ineffectiveness among investment professionals may be the relatively low incidence (compared with EA and ER) of such awards at corporate level. This issue is explored further below in section 3.3.

Table 3.1 Rating method for corporate environmental disclosures

Rating scale/environmental policy	Typical example
0. No disclosure	
1. General rhetoric	'Reuters is an environmentally aware organisation. Reuters journalists cover environmental issues as part of their regular activity' (Reuters)
2. Specific endeavour; policy only	'It is the Group's policy ... to minimise the potential for adverse effects of its operations through systematic and rigorous application of high standards and practices' (BOC)
3. Specific endeavour; policy specified	'Our policy is to comply with all relevant environmental standards.... We regularly recycle spent radioactive sources' (Amersham International)
4. Implementation and monitoring; use of targets, results not published	'To establish baseline data and help set targets and objectives, working parties have been set up to study our position' (Boots)
5. Implementation and monitoring; use of targets, results published	'Our capital investment on pollution abatement in 1993 was about £250m, compared with £350m in 1992. In 1994 and 1995 we expect the sums to be about £290m and £250m respectively' (BP)

Source: Sample company annual reports, 1993. For further examples, see Robertson and Nicholson (1996)

3.3 Trends in environmental management and environmental reporting

The first part of this discussion examines general trends in environmental accounting activities and disclosures. Disclosure scores derived from the taxonomy in Table 3.1 are examined first. Trends affecting other indicators of environmental management activities are then reviewed. In particular, environmental auditing, publication of separate environmental reports, and the use of Kitemarks for quality environmental management systems are reviewed.

3.3.1 Total disclosure scores

The general trend in corporate disclosure for the period 1993–7 is shown in Figure 3.1 and Table 3.2. Figure 3.1 shows the percentage of companies in the sample making environmental disclosures of any kind. Table 3.2 breaks down this total into the five qualitative categories of disclosure outlined above in Table 3.1.

There is an overall increase, from about 65 per cent to 80 per cent, in the number of companies making environmental disclosures of whatever sort. Gray et al. (1995) show that the major increase in voluntary disclosure took place in the period 1985 to 1991, when the increase for their sample was from under 10 per cent to over 70 per cent. The result here shows that the rising trend identified by Gray et al. has continued well into the 1990s. The sample for the latter is based on the 100 largest companies, whereas the current study is based on a sample drawn from approximately the largest 250. Differing samples may be one reason why the graph in Gray et al. (1995, p.58) cannot be directly extrapolated into the results from this survey. Also, as indicated by Gray et al. (n. 17, ibid.), the results before 1988 need to be treated with caution. For the other details in Table 3.2, there is no basis of direct comparison with other UK studies. As noted earlier, these concentrate on volume of disclosure, whereas the purpose here is to examine the quality signal inherent in the style of disclosure. In this respect, the findings in Table 3.2 are of some interest. The rising general trend (Figure 3.1) is accounted for by increases at both ends of the scale, with no clear trend in the middle values. Thus, there is a large increase in companies reporting at the level of general rhetoric, especially in the more recent period. Management considering the value of such disclosures should bear in mind the paucity of the information content from the point of view of the investment community. There is also a small but growing cadre of companies that report environmental results at the highest level, that is, published results against published targets.

Figure 3.1 Percentage of companies disclosing environmental information

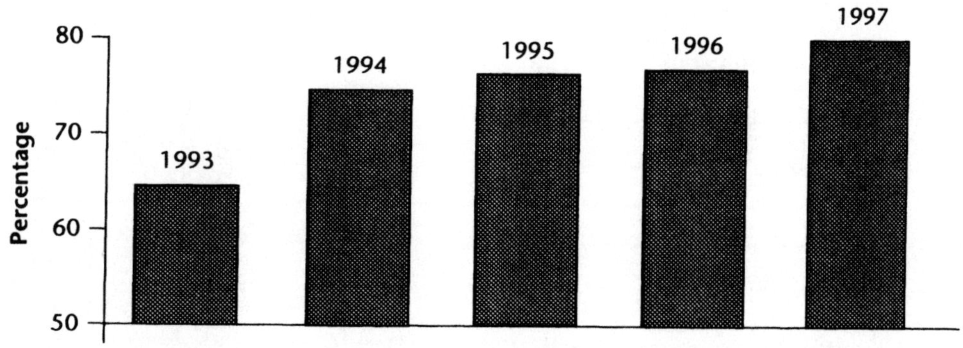

Table 3.2 Recent trends in UK corporate environmental disclosures, 1993–7

Year	No. of firms	Total	Disclosure rating (% disclosing) 5	4	3	2	1	0
1993	128	64.84	4.69	9.38	28.13	16.41	6.25	35.16
1994	116	75.00	4.31	11.21	32.76	18.97	7.76	25.00
1995	111	76.58	6.31	11.71	30.63	26.13	1.80	23.42
1996	172	77.33	5.81	11.05	31.40	17.44	11.63	22.67
1997	168	79.76	7.74	9.52	30.36	17.86	14.29	20.24
Overall	695	75.11	5.90	10.50	30.65	18.99	9.06	24.89

Source: Sample company annual reports

3.3.2 Kitemarks, environmental reports and environmental audits

Table 3.3 shows the achievement of KITES and use of environmental reports and audits for the full sample firms across 26 industry groups representing all major sectors of the UK economy. Kitemarks are shown as BS7750 (in force until 1995) and ISO14001, which has superseded the earlier British standard. Levels of ER and environmental auditing, internal (EA INT) and external (EA EXT), are also shown. Each is now discussed in turn.

ISO 14001 is intended as a voluntary response to the problems of international enforcement of environmental standards. It does not therefore require reporting, but in theory it may be one of the best ways of bringing a company's environmental management system (EMS) in line with best practice. As can be seen from Table 3.3, the take-up of ISO14001 has been very low for UK companies. A possible reason is that it is relatively new. Companies that previously possessed the equivalent UK KITE (BS7750) have transferred to the new award. However, there is no evidence that new companies are forwarding their EMS for scrutiny under this system. An alternative explanation is that these KITES are not recognised as a quality signal by the investment community. Evidence from Chapter 2 supports such a view. Advocates of ISO14001 have suggested that market forces, rather than regulation, will make the standard a precondition for trading globally. In the light of current UK trends, those who have already dismissed it as a failure appear to be well justified in their conclusions (Krut and Gleckman, 1998).

Table 3.3 Recent trends in UK corporate environmental management reporting, 1993–7

Year	No. of firms	KITES BS7750	KITES ISO14001	ER	EA INT	EA EXT
1993	128	0	0	3	2	0
1994	116	0	0	11	16	2
1995	111	2	0	16	17	2
1996	172	7	1	19	9	1
1997	168	1	6	9	10	4

Source: Sample company annual reports

In this small minority of cases, details of environmental performance are left out of the main annual report and included instead as a separate document. For the purposes of the disclosure rating system in Table 3.2, companies using this policy were assessed on the contents of the separate environmental report. It was assumed that this would give a more accurate representation of actual environmental policy, as opposed to how management choose to signal their activities to the markets. There was a rising trend in the issue of separate environmental reports in the period 1993–6. However, 1997 shows a significant fall in numbers of companies adopting this reporting strategy. Utility companies have been particularly prominent in the use of the ER. However, takeover and merger activity in the power and water sectors reduced the number of such companies in the sample in 1997. Another reason for the apparent decline was a tendency for companies that reported in 1996 to commit themselves to five-year targets, for example on waste and emissions. These promises were therefore accompanied by the announcement of an intermittent reporting cycle. Whether this reduction in accountability translates into improved performance through long-term commitment remains to be seen.

Turning to auditing, again the incidence has generally increased, although there is no discernible incremental trend. Companies using external environmental auditors remain a tiny minority (for example, Body Shop and Enterprise Oil). Of those using audits, a majority favour internal verification procedures as the dominant method. Some of this group use hybrid systems of accountability involving some external scrutiny, such as non-executive audit committees (for example, Thames Water) and external assessment of internal procedures (for example, BNFL, Caradon and Courtaulds Textiles), while others use intermittent cycles (for example, Pilkington, every three years). In Table 3.3 these have all been classified according to the dominant method, i.e. as internal audits. From the earlier research results in Chapter 2 there is a suggestion that the investment community places considerable emphasis on the additional credibility offered by audits. The actual level of use is therefore rather lower than might be expected.

3.4 Conclusions

The above survey has shown that the extent of environmental disclosure by UK companies continues to increase. There are several potential explanations of this trend towards rising disclosure. They fall under the broad headings of stakeholder 'push' and the 'pull' of financial incentives. In the former category are the impacts of regulatory changes and the monitoring actions of pressure groups. In the latter is the hypothesis that there is a financial dividend to environmental action.

In all the above areas of disclosure, and, indeed, for the issue of environmental reporting more generally, there is some evidence of managerial resistance to the process. As was shown in Table 3.2, notwithstanding the rising trend of environmental reporting observed in this and previous surveys, a significant minority of companies continue to ignore the issue. Corporate management has offered some possible reasons, according to the views expressed in one discussion of environmental reports. Their reasons for non-reporting included (*Environmental Accounting and Auditing Reporter,* 1998): 'we have doubts about the advantages it would bring to our company'; 'it's too expensive'; and 'it would not increase our sales'.

The points are also relevant to the more general disclosure issue. These objections suggest that there will be a certain degree of managerial inertia unless significant pressures and incentives are applied. The analytical survey in the next section investigates further what these pressures might be.

Key points are that:

- In the very near future the inclusion of environmental information of some kind will be expected as standard for most large UK plcs.
- The quality of environmental disclosure is increasing.
- The annual report is a more widely used and strategic means of communication than a separate environmental report.
- Environmental auditing is not commonplace and is probably below the expectation level of the investment community.
- Very few firms have responded to the opportunities offered by Kitemark schemes.

4

Determinants of Environmental Disclosure

The previous chapter showed that there is a rising trend in certain aspects of environmental disclosure within annual reports. Some companies are clearly more concerned to report their environmental performance than are others. In this chapter the reasons for these variations are explored.

The approach adopted below is to examine the relationship between managerial action and shareholder response. Accordingly, if shareholders perceive the environment to be irrelevant, there should be no association between disclosure and the variables analysed. These are the prior profitability of the firm, the dispersion of share ownership, systematic risk and level of borrowing. It is also supposed that the actions of lobby groups and government regulators are important to shareholders where their actions might be anticipated to affect share price. Within this framework, management is assumed to signal the quality of their environmental management procedures via environmental report disclosures. As suggested in Chapter 1, the model is therefore referred to as the extended single stakeholder model of disclosure. For reasons discussed in the previous two chapters, an objective of the survey was to measure the qualitative level of accountability represented by the disclosures. This scale was then used in statistical models that attempt to replicate some of the significant US studies carried out over recent years. These models are not reproduced in full below, but the associations they suggest are commented upon. The interested reader is referred to the original CIMA report, *Financial Performance Differentials in 'Ethically' Managed Companies*. There have been very few analytical studies of this kind previously conducted using UK data. As part of the analysis, the survey also seeks to offer explanations for the underlying increase observed during the period and discussed in Chapter 3. It also considers specific industries and hence the nature of the companies' activities, and thereby also aims to explain variations in management and accounting practice within the UK economy.

4.1 Possible reasons for increasing disclosure

Increasing regulation is likely to push companies towards increasing environmental disclosure. Where capital market participants anticipate regulatory developments, investor pressures could also drive corporate managers to adopt pre-emptive measures. It is probably also true that the larger firm will be more likely to respond to the pressures of such scrutiny. Previous empirical studies in the USA have suggested that company size is an important determinant of environmental disclosure (for example, Trotman and Bradley, 1981; Patten, 1991). Another case may be where there are creditor groups vulnerable to managerial actions that may increase their perceived risk (Barton, et al., 1989; Roberts, 1992). An example would be only minimal compliance with environmental regulation. Others have argued that the nature of the industry is more important to the information content of social responsibility disclosures (Ingram, 1978). This may be a function of exposure to particular activities within the product range: for example, the degree to which the company's activities modify the environment (Dierkes and Preston, 1977). More specifically, it may refer to the proximity to the customer within the value chain. Such a view assumes that pressure for corporate environmental sensitivity comes from consumer preference, and that those firms that are closer to the final consumer are more vulnerable to such pressures (Cowen et al., 1987). Another argument is that prior profitability influences disclosure. It may be, for example, that profitable companies possess greater free cash flow and hence the opportunity to make investments in social and environmental projects. It may also be true that good-quality management teams can simultaneously generate good profits and make sensible investments in environmental projects. Alternatively, in periods of poor profitability, management may seek to distract attention from questions about their financial competence by drawing attention to environmental projects. Research in the USA has shown that managers tend to disclose qualitative 'good news' and quantitative 'bad news' simultaneously (Gibbins et al., 1990). Finally, some researchers have reported a positive association between environmental disclosures and higher systematic risk. For evidence on prior profitability and systematic risk, see Trotman and Bradley (1981), Cowen et al. (1987), and Neu et al. (1998).

Most of these conclusions are based on empirical tests in one form or another. However, they are difficult to interpret because they have used different populations of firms, or have been confined to particular industries. For example, Bowman and Haire (1975) considered only companies in the US food-processing industry. The majority have used US data, although there have also been some European surveys. As noted in Chapter 3, UK surveys have concentrated on the actual level and characteristics of environmental disclosure. Meanwhile, in contrast to the USA, few of them have considered models of causation or association to explain the presence of environmental disclosures within annual reports. This is the main purpose of the survey that follows.

4.2 Survey design

The rating system introduced in Chapter 3 (see Table 3.1) was used as the explained variable in a series of regression models, and a series of independent variables were identified based on the results of the studies referred to above. These models are documented fully in the associated research report. In the ensuing narrative, the impact of each variable on the qualitative level of environmental disclosure is illustrated in a series of figures.

To examine the relationship between financial stakeholders and the conduct and disclosure of environmental management activities, four proxy variables were used. Firstly, block shareholdings were measured. Blocks were defined as the combined ownership percentage of significant investors (with a holding of more than 3 per cent) and directors. In a US study Roberts (1992) used a similar variable with a threshold of 5 per cent. Here, 3 per cent is used as being the disclosure threshold for UK corporate reporting and the level available from Datastream. For each company, the blocks over 3 per cent were totalled. That total percentage is labelled BLOCK in the figures below. Where shareholding is dispersed, it is expected that the demands placed on managers would become broader. Hence, pressure from financial stakeholders would lead to more disclosure (Keim, 1978; Roberts, 1992). This view also follows from the general discussion in Chapter 1. Further, dispersed shareholders face higher moral hazard and adverse selection risks, and, accordingly, management has a greater incentive to engage in quality signalling disclosures. This is especially the case where market participants equate environmental responsibility with good management (Alexander and Buchholz, 1978; Spicer, 1978).

If this were true, such firms might also be expected to enjoy lower systematic risk and hence access to cheaper capital. Thus, a second variable examined was the beta factor (BETA). Another reason why companies with high environmental responsibility might have lower systematic risk is that stable returns provide the opportunity for managers to participate in environmentally responsible projects. Recall from Chapter 2 that investment analysts in particular regarded good environmental management as a risk-reducing activity. Conversely, where a new project is high risk, or in an environmentally sensitive area, managers might have an incentive to signal to the market to reassure investors. The predicted relationship between beta and environmental disclosure is not therefore obvious. This is apparent in the contradictory results from previous empirical surveys. Similarly, as noted earlier, many previous studies have used prior profitability to measure the influence of financial stakeholders. Here, in parallel with a significant US survey, this is measured by average return on equity (ROE) in the three years prior to disclosure (Cowen et al., 1987). As with the current study, this survey contrasted disclosures across a similar number of industry groups and simultaneously examined the effects of firm size. It is therefore sensible to use a consistent variable in the present study. Again the empirical evidence is mixed, and the expected sign on the ROE coefficient is not obvious.

A final financial stakeholder variable is the level of financial gearing. This is defined as the ratio of long-term debt to shareholders' equity (GEAR). It measures the interests of third-party financial stakeholders. Again, the expected nature of the relationship is not obvious. Studies of accounting choice have suggested that a high level of gearing is related to changes in accounting practice. However, these studies have been limited to those practices that impact directly on bottom-line reported earnings (see, for example, Watts and Zimmermann, 1986). Environmental disclosures, as noted already, are under-theorised in this respect. Some have argued that where stakeholder management is practised, a positive relationship will be observed between borrowings and disclosures (for example, Barton et al., 1989; Roberts, 1992). On the other hand, where outstanding borrowings are high in relation to the asset base, default risk is higher and therefore management may be reluctant to make additional investments, especially where project risk cannot be clearly evaluated. In environmentally sensitive industries, such firms may therefore do the minimum necessary to comply with regulations. In other industries, they may make no environmental investments at all. Such investment may also be a function of limited free cash flow in heavily borrowed firms (per the 'free cash flow' hypothesis, Jensen, 1986). In the light of these competing theories, and the absence of a large body of evidence on green accounting choice from prior studies, the relationship between borrowing and environmental disclosure remains an empirical question.

In addition to financial stakeholders, in the light of the discussion above, it was also considered useful to examine the impact of size. This is measured in the figures below by the natural log of sales revenue (SIZE). The potential environmental sensitivity of activities the company may be involved in suggested that industry sector should also be taken into account. Most previous studies have either concentrated on industries thought to be environmentally sensitive, or have attempted to control for cross-sectional variation where using more general samples. For a recent example of the former, see Neu et al. (1998); for an example of the latter, see Cowen et al. (1987). Roberts (1992) summarises methods of identifying industries in previous surveys as *ad hoc*. As discussed earlier, there are a number of reasons why environmental management and hence disclosures might be expected to vary from industry to industry. Here, for direct evidence of the degree of environmental sensitivity and the degree of managerial engagement with environmental issues, the level of environmental capital expenditure was used. As Figure 4.1 shows, a Department of the Environment survey found that 69 per cent of environmental capital expenditure was accounted for by six industries. These were: chemicals, food processing (food), paper and pulp (paper), minerals processing, taken for the purposes of this study to include building and aggregates (building), energy supply, for the purposes of this study all utilities, including water (energy), metals manufacture (metals), rubber and plastics (rubber). Figure 4.1 shows the percentage of total environmental capital expenditure accounted for by each industry.

For the purposes of the current study, the industries in Figure 4.1 were defined as environmentally sensitive (ES). Given the levels of expenditure, it is also expected that the level of disclosure should also be high for these industries.

Information for all financial variables was obtained from Datastream. Industry criteria (ES) were assigned to each company in the sample from analysis of sales by product and the SIC code taken from Datastream. The SIC codes corresponded to those used in the DoE survey discussed above. If any of the company's product sales fell under an ES SIC code the company was put into the ES group, or put into the non-ES group otherwise. Betas were obtained from the London Business School Risk Measurement Service.

Figure 4.1 Capital expenditure on the environment by industry

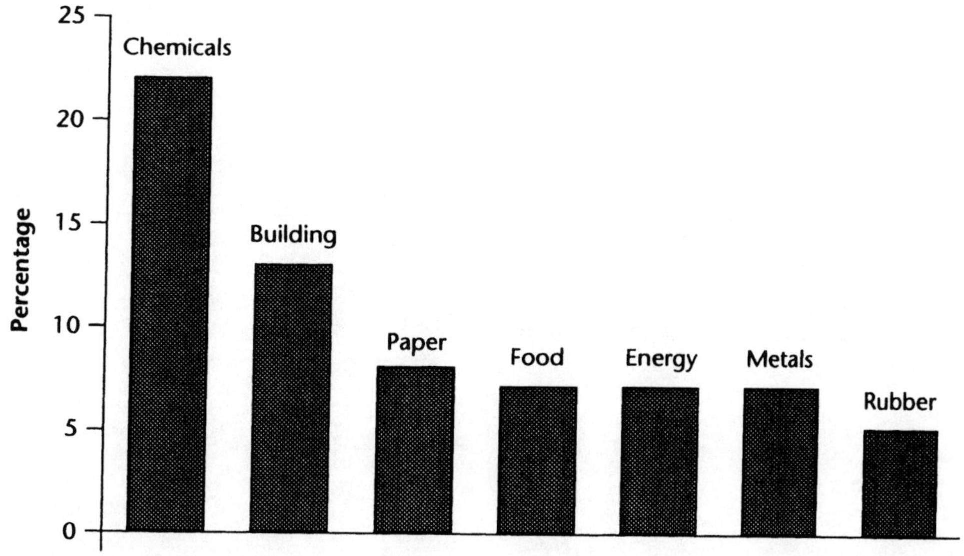

Source: Adapted from Department of Environment (1996)

4.3 Analysis of results

The discussion below examines the impact of contingency factors on environmental disclosure policy. There are two aspects to this. The first deals with the quality of disclosure using the rating scale devised in Chapter 3. The second examines the determinants of the decision to disclose any information at all. Each aspect is now discussed in more detail.

Table 4.1 shows means and standard deviations (SDs) for each variable by class of environmental disclosure, using the quality rating scale from Table 3.1. This allows a comparison to be made between the characteristics of companies that are able to report qualitatively different environmental policies.

Table 4.1 Statistical attributes of each variable

Disclosure class		BETA	BLOCK	ROE	GEAR	LOG SIZE
5	Mean	0.912	16.993	23.579	0.367	15.062
	SD	0.136	14.156	7.7298	0.239	1.3673
4	Mean	1.019	16.058	16.308	0.420	14.786
	SD	0.200	15.153	7.1961	0.327	1.1783
3	Mean	0.994	21.714	15.284	0.547	14.430
	SD	0.196	17.947	13.141	0.749	1.1101
2	Mean	1.059	22.550	17.781	0.495	14.357
	SD	0.188	18.169	12.600	0.408	1.3929
1	Mean	0.953	26.489	19.905	1.314	13.561
	SD	0.213	15.966	18.783	2.195	1.3387
0	Mean	1.009	32.425	15.324	0.516	13.544
	SD	0.183	22.011	13.750	0.619	1.5470

As can be seen from Table 4.1, there are no clear trends for ROE, GEAR and BETA. Some reasons for this are examined below. The BLOCK and SIZE variables, however, suggest an apparent set of relationships. Figures 4.2 and 4.3 illustrate the trends for these two variables.

4.3.1 Block shareholdings

Figure 4.2 shows the effect of block shareholdings on the quality of disclosure. The vertical scale is the sum of all blocks greater than 3 per cent, and quality of disclosure is measured by the scale discussed in Chapter 3 (see Table 3.1).

Figure 4.2 Block shareholding and environmental disclosure quality

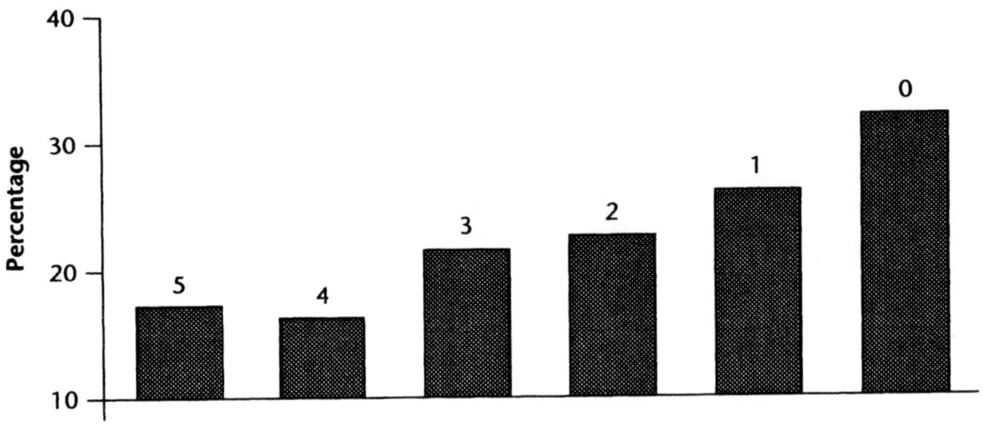

As the graph illustrates, there was a clear trend towards lower-quality disclosures in the sample companies where larger block shareholdings prevailed. In other words, it is suggested that companies with more diverse shareholdings have better-quality environmental disclosures. A likely reason is that diversely owned corporations are subject to greater scrutiny from the capital markets. Within environmentally sensitive industries, BLOCK was important for energy, but less so for food processing, chemical and rubber and plastics companies. Block shareholdings also made it less likely that companies would disclose any environmental information at all. In general, these findings support the predictions of the extended single stakeholder model discussed earlier. The evidence thus supports the notion that capital markets scrutinise and interpret the actions of management and outside stakeholders with recognition of the potential impacts of lobby groups and regulation on share price.

4.3.2 Firm size

Figure 4.3 illustrates the impact of firm size on disclosure policy. Size is measured on the vertical axis by sales revenue.

Figure 4.3 Firm size and environmental disclosure quality

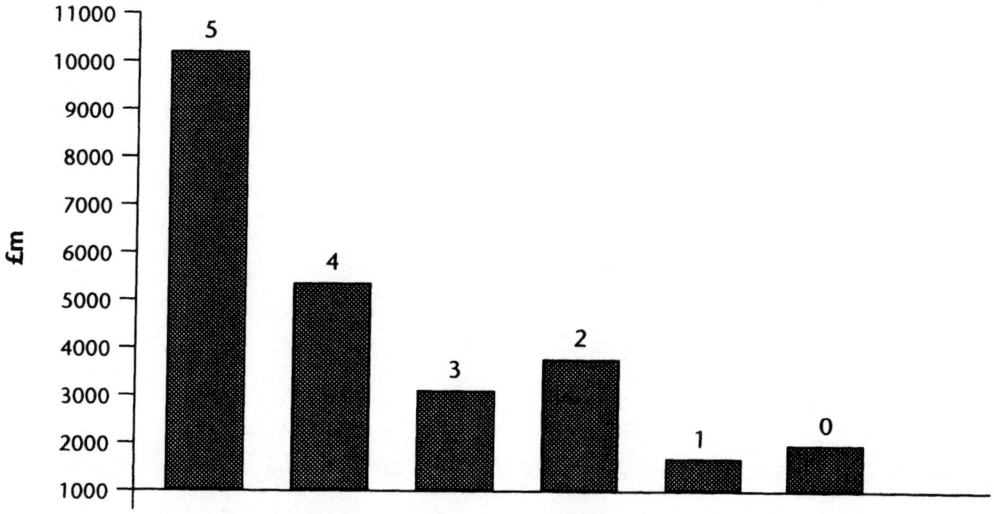

As can be seen in Figure 4.3, size had a clear and strong influence on the quality of disclosure within the sample companies. Large firms were particularly associated with the publication of quantitative targets and monitoring performance against them. Some of these firms are either former public sector or in any case subject to stronger regulatory pressures. Firm size also had a significant impact on the decision to disclose any environmental information at all. However, not all the large companies in the sample were subject to these accountability structures, and some of the relationship may also be due to the higher public profile of the larger firm. This seems very likely, as larger firms might face greater capital market scrutiny. Diverse share ownership, as we have seen, is also associated with improved environmental accountability. Relatively few firms achieved ratings of 5 in the qualitative survey for both 1996 and 1997. These are listed in Table 4.2.

Table 4.2 Sample firms with consecutively highly rated environmental disclosures, 1996–7

British Petroleum
National Power
Powergen
Smithkline Beecham
Southern Electric
Zeneca

Source: Annual reports

Firms that improved their ratings from lower levels in prior years but obtaining ratings of 5 in 1997 included Body Shop, Courtaulds and Scottish Power. The case of Body Shop and its annual report is interesting. It has pursued a prominent business strategy based on its environmental profile for a number of years, yet the company has only recently begun to disclose performance against quantifiable targets. In a way this is not surprising because, as can be seen, such a style of reporting is confined to a relatively small group of large firms. None the less, it should be recalled that this kind of quantitative evidence is precisely the type that is most likely to convince interested investment professionals about genuine environmental performance. Of the larger firms, some are subject to direct regulation from government watchdogs such as OFFER and the Environment Agency. Smithkline Beecham's disclosure strategy appears exceptional, since it is not included in any of the environmentally sensitive industry sectors defined earlier according to levels of environmental expenditure (Figure 4.1). However, it does have a significant involvement in the more tightly regulated US market, and this may influence the disclosure strategy for the company as a whole.

4.3.3 Financial structure

Corporate borrowing had a mixed impact on the disclosure activities of companies in the sample. Figure 4.4 summarises the results and, as can be seen, there was a tendency for lower dependence on debt finance to improve the quality of environmental disclosure among the sample companies. More prominent, however, was the tendency for very heavily borrowed firms to engage in general rhetoric about the environment. This apparently odd trend is partly explained by the role of companies in the media sector. These companies tend to have significant intangible (and off balance-sheet assets) and hence disproportionately high gearing ratios. At the same time, their management does not view the environment as an important strategic variable but may, because of the nature of the business, be aware of its potential propaganda weapon. Carlton, Daily Mail, Granada, Mirror Group and Pearson are examples of highly geared media companies with disclosure at the level of rhetoric or no disclosure at all. However, the effect is not entirely confined to one sector. ICI and Rentokil are other examples of large and highly geared firms disclosing at the rhetoric level.

At a more general level, it is possible that heavily borrowed companies have little free cash flow to engage in significant environmental expenditure. Therefore, although they disclose environmental information to conform to industry norms, they do so at the level of rhetoric rather than monitoring and implementation. Low-level disclosures may be used to reassure borrowers about the competence of managers and the perceived risk of environmental projects. Hence, borrowing might create stakeholder pressure to disclose some information but not to increase the quality of disclosure. Other surveys, using US data (for example, Roberts, 1992), have found weak but positive associations between borrowing and social disclosures and concluded that disclosure is a useful mechanism in meeting creditor expectations. Those results are contradicted in the current survey, although it should be borne in mind that the conclusions here are confined to environmental disclosures only. None the less, further research into this relationship is required.

Figure 4.4 Corporate borrowing and environmental disclosure quality

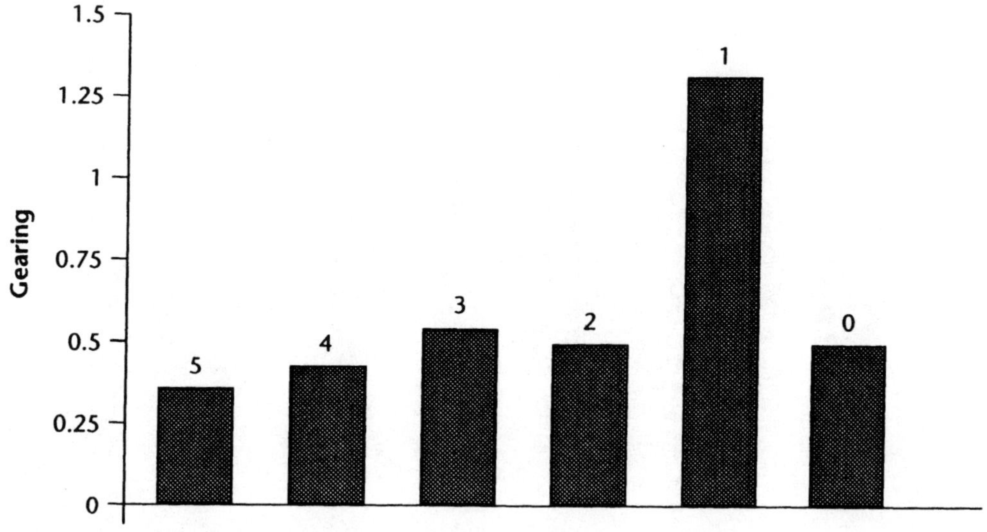

4.3.4 Industry effects

Another important result from the survey was the impact of industry norms on disclosure policies. The main trends are illustrated in Figure 4.5. In all industries identified as environmentally sensitive, there was a significant differential in quality of environmental reporting. The only exception was rubber and plastics, whose average score was similar to non-environmentally sensitive industries. Membership of the ES group of industries also had a significant impact on the decision to disclose at all. In a similar US survey, there were only limited industry effects. Of the industries considered in the current survey, only membership of the paper and chemicals industries were found to be significant as determinants of disclosure in the USA in the mid-1980s (Cowen et al., 1987). Another prior survey also observed a significant relationship between industry profile and rating of corporate social disclosures (Roberts, 1992). In the UK, disclosure practices in the chemical industry reflect a greater degree of voluntarism than in the more heavily regulated United States. Voluntary codes of practice, such as that developed by the Chemical Industries Association, may explain the high quality of disclosure in that industry suggested by Figure 4.5. Companies included in the UK energy sector, by contrast, reflect the regulatory pressures of watchdog-dominated privatised utilities.

Figure 4.5 Industry sector influences on environmental disclosure quality

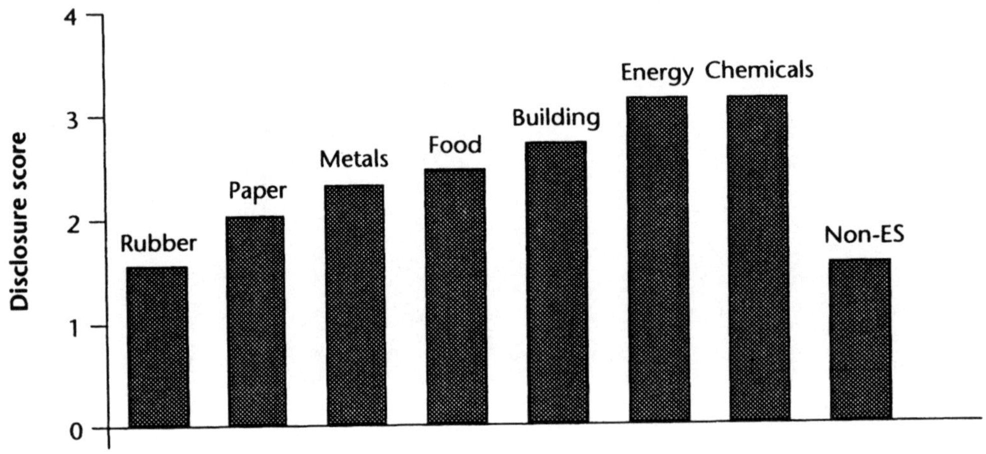

4.3.5 Other factors

There were no cases in which systematic risk, measured by beta, displayed any significant association with the level of disclosure or the mere act of disclosure (Table 4.1). This contradicts the findings of previous studies, and, to an extent, the findings in Chapter 2 that showed that investment professionals equated environmental responsibility with lower risk. Other surveys have shown that companies with higher systematic risk are less likely to commit resources to and therefore disclose social and environmental activities. A study that concentrated exclusively on pollution control found a similar relationship, although it became weaker through time, attributed to an overall improvement in the pollution control records of all sample companies. Spicer's (1978) study examined practices in the paper and pulp industry, and for comparable findings see also McGuire et al. (1988) and Roberts (1992). As shown above, it is true that similar processes are affecting UK companies in environmentally sensitive industries. It may also be the case that the effects of quality signalling, for example where risky environmental investments are required, offset the association of good management and lower risk. Clearly, however, further research into the relationship between systematic risk and environmental disclosure in the UK is required.

Prior and current profitability (ROE) also had no effect in any model of either type. Again, brief inspection of Table 4.1 shows no evidence of a trend. Research on US data has shown that prior profitability is an important determinant of social disclosure (Roberts, 1992). A possible reason for the differing conclusions here is that the current concern is with environmental responsibility only; other social concerns have not been measured by the disclosure ratings in this research. Studies that have examined the impacts of pollution alone, such as the CEP ratings in the USA, have observed a U-shaped relationship between corporate social responsibility and financial performance (Bragdon and Marlin, 1972; Bowman and Haire, 1975). The 'U-shaped private cost model' suggests that investment in environmental projects improve ROE towards a 'golden mean', but that after this point is reached the costs of environmental improvement outweigh the financial benefits. From Table 4.1, ROE appears weakly but positively related to quality of environmental disclosure. Those with the strongest commitment to environmental management and accountability perform well, and appear to have strong *ex ante* cash flow as measured by ROE. Those in the middle are relatively less profitable. The non-linear pattern would also explain the poor performance of this variable in statistical tests of association. Another possibility is that profits and positive free cash flow are counteracted by the qualitative 'good news' and quantitative 'bad news' disclosure effect referred to in section 4.2 above (Gibbins et al., 1990). None the less, in the light of these results, the conclusions suggested earlier that free cash flow explains higher levels of environmental activity and disclosure should be treated with caution. Again, further research is needed on this relationship. However, it is possible to infer at this stage that good financial performance does not confer a 'halo' of perceived environmental performance. This will be investigated further when the issue of environmental reputation is examined in the next chapter.

4.4 Conclusions

The results of the empirical tests reveal three particularly interesting aspects. Industry group, size and dispersed shareholdings are positively and strongly associated with the disclosure of environmental information and with the level and quality of those disclosures. Thus large companies, in environmentally sensitive industries with dispersed ownership, are more likely to provide details of implementation environmental strategies, details of performance against target, and details of specific environmental policies. Other firms are more likely to engage in mere environmental rhetoric or not disclose details of environmental issues at all. For the former group, in the light of the quantitative and observable nature of their disclosures, it is likely that the content of annual reports mirrors closely their actual policies. Another interesting aspect of the results is that prior economic performance and measures of stakeholder power (excluding shareholders) offer little explanation of disclosure practices. One interpretation of the trends is that managerial actions are dictated by exposure to public, regulator and capital market scrutiny, a central prediction of the extended stakeholder model. Other non-shareholder influences are not extensively tested here, although levels of borrowing do not appear to reflect pressures from third-party stakeholders to disclose environmental policies. There are, therefore, some caveats associated with the number of independent variables tested. None the less, these results form the basis for further research to examine associations between environmental disclosures and environmental reputation and also between disclosure, reputation and financial performance.

Key points are that:

- Non-family-owned firms with dispersed share ownership have higher-quality environmental disclosures.
- Larger firms have higher-quality environmental disclosures.
- Capital expenditure on environmental projects is associated with higher-

quality disclosure in environmentally sensitive industries. Industry norms and voluntary codes of practice may also drive such disclosures.

- Environmental disclosure does not increase in response to greater use of debt finance or higher systematic risk.
- Environmental disclosure does not increase in response to *ex ante* profitability and hence cash flow.

5

Determinants of Corporate Environmental Reputation

The objective of this chapter is to investigate the mechanisms available to management for the creation of corporate environmental reputation. These mechanisms are primarily the disclosure and signalling devices identified as important to investment professionals and investigated in previous chapters. The relationship between these signalling disclosure strategies and environmental reputation is tested below on a sample of UK public limited companies.

To measure reputation this analysis uses data from the UK 'Most Admired Companies' (MAC) surveys. For a number of years, first in the USA and subsequently in the UK, surveys have sought to provide a rating for corporate reputation, including a rating for community and environmental responsibility. These MAC surveys are published annually in *Fortune* (USA) and *Management Today* (UK) respectively. Empirical results from these surveys have been treated with scepticism in some quarters. Whatever the justification for such scepticism, if, as the results in US empirical surveys suggest, the market imputes value to the published results then there are undeniable consequences for management. In particular, executives will need to pay careful attention to their year-to-year position in the corporate reputation league tables. It may follow that, in the same way that management has traditionally concentrated a great deal on the costs and benefits of investment in physical assets, it must now extend its efforts to the less tangible aspects of the businesses. Moreover, the existence of an environmental responsibility league table provides the opportunity to examine how reputations are established and whether such a league table is a valid yardstick of actual management policy. These are the principal objectives of this chapter.

5.1 Environmental accounting and environmental reputation

Environmental management for many firms is likely to be an important ingredient of general reputation. This will become truer in the future to the extent that the environment moves up the political and regulatory agenda. However, investment in reputation is difficult to manage since it is also difficult to measure and to value. The reputation of a business might be considered the most intangible of intangible assets. Accounting practice provides little direction on the valuation of these goodwill-based assets and, as a result, there are significant variations in accounting-based disclosures. Similarly, where some of the payback of new capital investment is in goodwill assets such as reputation, the benefits will typically remain imprecise for internal decision-makers. None the less, as suggested in the introductory discussion in Chapter 1, there is evidence to suggest that reputation is becoming a more important driver of competitive advantage.

Managers aspiring to excellence in environmental management face more complex processes than when applying their strategies in other fields. Product development, for example, can be communicated to the customer stakeholder group via price and advertising information, new work practices via employee training etc. Improved environmental practice – for example, an investment in cleaner technology – will count for little if its purpose is not communicated effectively outside the organisation. Moreover, such announcements, as with advertising, are not simply a matter of established practices and channels of communication. In some industries, there is a risk that the greatest diligence in environmental practice will not be believed by the external stakeholder groups upon which the ultimate survival of the organisation depends. Conversely, it might be possible for some organisations to create a reputation for good environmental performance on the basis of relatively superficial managerial strategies. Such actions may only compound the difficulties of the genuinely committed firm.

A crucial aspect of environmental performance is therefore not merely the act of investment itself, but also how those strategies are communicated. The purpose of this chapter is to examine the relationship between corporate environmental strategies, as communicated via accounting disclosures, and environmental reputation. As already suggested, it is difficult to observe the actual environmental performance of a business. The association of environmental disclosure and environmental performance is therefore overwhelmingly an empirical question. An exception is the contingency framework proposed by Ullmann (1985). Here, social (which can be taken to include environmental) performance and disclosures are contingencies to manage dependence relationships. Dependency has three dimensions. First, where stakeholder power is high, social disclosure is also predicted to be high. In the UK context, there is some empirical support for this relationship (Chapter 4). Second, strategic posture influences the organisation's relationship with its stakeholders. Strategic posture refers to the ways in which managers seek to influence the organisation's relationship with important stakeholders. The impact on social performance and social disclosure depends on interaction with the first and third variables. The third variable is economic performance. For the development of testable hypotheses, the present concern is with only a modified segment of Ullmann's model (as set out in Table 5.1 overleaf). Here the part of the model that distinguishes between voluntary and mandated disclosure is omitted, since in the UK the framework is almost entirely voluntary. In addition, variables can interact to produce an indeterminate social and social disclosure strategy, and these are also ignored at the hypothesis development stage of the current research. Table 5.1 therefore only shows hypothesised relationships between the three contingencies and strategy in a constrained set of circumstances. For reasons made clear in the ensuing discussion, Ullmann's model is very useful for testing corporate environmental disclosure and performance in the UK context. This is partly because there are few alternative competing models. None the less, the framework is useful, given the data constraints in testing these relationships in the UK context. In the following discussion, environmental performance is taken to imply environmental reputation.

Table 5.1 A contingency model of environmental performance and environmental disclosure

Stakeholder power	Strategic posture	Economic performance	Strategy
High	Active	Good	Environmental performance: High Environmental disclosure: High
High	Passive	Good	Environmental performance: High Environmental disclosure: Low
High	Passive	Poor	Environmental performance: Indeterminate Environmental disclosure: Low
Low	Active	Poor	Environmental performance: Low Environmental disclosure: Low
Low	Passive	Good	Environmental performance: Low Environmental disclosure: Low
Low	Passive	Poor	Environmental performance: Low Environmental disclosure: Low

Source: Adapted from Ullmann (1985)

Bearing in mind the difficulties in observing actual environmental performance (and therefore reputation), it would be convenient if there were a relationship between environmental disclosure and environmental performance. This would also facilitate the testing of the relationship between environmental performance and economic performance. However, as Ullmann puts it, 'Given the hypothetical character of the relationship between social performance and social disclosure, social disclosure cannot be substituted for social performance without prior empirical verification no matter how impressive the quantity and quality of the disclosed information' (1985, p. 541). Accordingly, it is the purpose of this chapter to establish the extent of such a relationship. If one exists, disclosure could then substitute as an empirical proxy for actual performance in future research. If not, it will be necessary to rely upon alternative measures. For the purposes of the current study, the remainder of the chapter examines the relationship between environmental disclosure and environmental reputation. Chapter 6 then goes on to consider the relationship between reputation and financial performance.

Until the mid-1980s, much of the research into this relationship was empirically based. Its results generally suggested little association between disclosure and actual environmental performance. These studies measured the actual environmental performance of US corporations by reference to the CEP ratings and disclosure by means of content analysis in most cases (for a summary of pre-1985 research, see Ullmann, 1985). Whatever the measure employed, the overall conclusion of no relationship between disclosure and actual social performance was consistent with the earlier studies. None the less, there has been recognition that reliance on mere number of disclosures may be misleading (Rockness, 1985). It is therefore appropriate, as discussed below, to develop more meaningful mechanisms for the interpretation of environmental performance.

Notwithstanding the general problem of measuring disclosure, US-based empirical surveys are difficult to replicate, given their reliance on data from monitoring agencies such as the CEP. In the UK there is no equivalent system of rating polluting activities by corporations. In the USA, as far as accounting disclosure is concerned, quoted companies are required to comply with SEC regulations. These include disclosure of the material effect of compliance with federal and state environmental laws on capital expenditure, earnings and competitive position, together with disclosure of future environmental expenditure (Regulation S-K, Item 101). In addition, since 1989 (SEC Release 6835) the SEC has required the disclosure of potential liabilities arising from environmental problems. All these developments subject the large US corporation to a potentially greater degree of scrutiny, and hence litigation, than comparable UK companies. In the UK, it might therefore be expected that voluntary disclosures by companies might be more self-congratulatory and be less reliable than in the USA. It was for this reason that the scoring system for measuring disclosure, discussed elsewhere (Chapter 4), penalises rhetoric and rewards the quantifiable and the verifiable.

While environmental disclosures appear unrelated to actual environmental performance in prior research, many of the empirical surveys conducted in the 1980s found other mediating influences on disclosure. These were specific firm characteristics and external influences. In particular, firm size and industry grouping provide a proxy for the degree of public pressure. Larger firms, higher systematic risk, industry and longer-term managerial decision horizon are associated with greater environmental disclosure, with size being particularly important in a significant number of studies (Patten, 1991; Trotman and Bradley, 1981; Wiseman, 1982; Cowen et al., 1987). For UK companies, as Chapter 4 revealed, size and industry grouping were also found to be highly significant. Systematic risk and prior profitability were less important.

Another important difference between this and previous US studies is the choice of explained variable. As pointed out earlier, US surveys are able to rely on published data for government agencies such as the CEP, for which no comparable UK database exists. Notwithstanding the availability of CEP data, some US studies have none the less used other variables. Reputation-based measures are principal among these (Fry and Hock, 1976; Preston, 1978; Abbot and Monsen, 1979).

Reputation viewed as an intangible business asset, as discussed in Chapter 1, is consistent with the resource-based view of the firm. This interpretation suggests that management quality and reputation will lead to competitive advantage and superior performance. Management quality is an important influence in fund managers' share selection decisions, and there is some evidence that managers can successfully signal perceptions of quality to the market. Chakravarthy (1986) found no relationship between managerial excellence and financial performance. McGuire et al. (1988) confirmed this result, but with reference only to the firm's social responsibility reputation. Fombrun and Shanley (1990) in turn contradicted their conclusions. However, in US empirical surveys, there is no convincing evidence of any relationship between social performance and financial performance. In the US research, a series of empirical examinations has also failed to identify a consistent relationship between apparent managerial excellence in several criteria and financial performance (McGuire et al., 1990). However, in one survey, prior financial performance, measured by risk and return, is associated with subsequent perceptions of firm quality reported in the *Fortune* MAC results (McGuire et al., 1990). In the same survey, when reputation scores are examined as determinants of financial performance, the relationship was found to be much weaker. Differences in choices of variable to represent both reputation and financial performance may be a possible reason for the lack of consensus in these results. As far as measures of financial performance are concerned, some use accounting-based measures, others stock-market-based measures.

A further problem contradicting the resource-based view of the firm, however, is that the MAC data is confounded by the so-called 'halo effect' (McGuire et al., 1988; Brown and Perry, 1994). With reference to empirical results on the parallel US admired companies data published in *Fortune,* the halo effect is the association of reputation scores with prior financial performance. If such an effect is also present for the UK data, then it is more problematic to rely on such data for the testing of research hypotheses. However, no such empirical test has yet been conducted using the UK scores. A further objective of the present study is to test for the existence of a halo effect.

Another weakness of the MAC survey method is that it may confound the true factors underlying superior performance. The MAC surveys use nine variables: quality of management, financial soundness, quality of products, ability to attract and retain top talent, value as a long-term investment, capacity to innovate, use of corporate assets, community and environmental responsibility, and quality of marketing. Not surprisingly, co-variances between these are high (see Fryxell and Wang, 1994). For current purposes, however, the most significant result was that the community and environmental responsibility variable was excepted from these overlapping effects (see Fryxell and Wang, 1994). The implication is that community and environmental strategies represent a distinct set of managerial tools for the creation of either corporate reputation or competitive advantage or both. It is the overall objective of this research to establish the true nature of these relationships.

5.2 Survey design

In the light of the above discussion, data was collected for several groups of variables for all the companies in the sample. These are listed in Table 5.2.

Table 5.2 Definitions of variables

CER	Corporate environmental reputation as measured by the community and environmental responsibility rating for the *Management Today* survey of 'Britain's Most Admired Companies'.
DISC	Disclosure score, ranging from 0 = no disclosure to 5 = high-quality disclosure.
KITE	Companies were included in this group if they had obtained an environmental quality Kitemark and were excluded otherwise.
ENVR	Companies were included in this group if they publish a separate environmental report, and were excluded otherwise.
ENVA	Companies were included in this group if they were subject to an environmental audit, and were excluded otherwise.
BETA	Systematic risk as measured by the company's beta factor.
PROFIT	Average return on equity (ROE) for the previous three years.
SIZE	Company size measured by the natural logarithm of sales turnover.
IND	Companies were included in this group if any of their activities fell under the same SIC code as an ES industry (as defined in Chapter 4, Figure 4.1), and were excluded otherwise.
BLOCK	Power of shareholders: the total percentage of shareholder groups with a stake of more than 3 per cent plus directors' shareholdings.

To measure CER, data was collected from the UK MACs for 1996 and 1997. The DISC variable was per the scale defined previously in Table 3.1. Companies were assigned to the KITES group for any Kitemark obtained by any subsidiary within the group, and included cases where there was more than one Kitemark within the corporate structure. In all cases these were either BS7750, ISO14001 or in the ISO9000 quality management series. The existence of ENVR was ascertained by reference to the main annual report of each company. ENVA was defined as either internal or external audit. Data for ROE, BLOCK and SIZE was obtained from Datastream for each company. BETA was obtained from the London Business School Risk Measurement Service.

5.3 Analysis of results

5.3.1 Industry effects

Before considering firm-specific variables, it is useful to examine how disclosure and reputation vary across industry. Figure 5.1 illustrates the relationship. This gives a further perspective, in addition to the ES version of the IND variable discussed so far.

Figure 5.1 Disclosure and reputation by industry

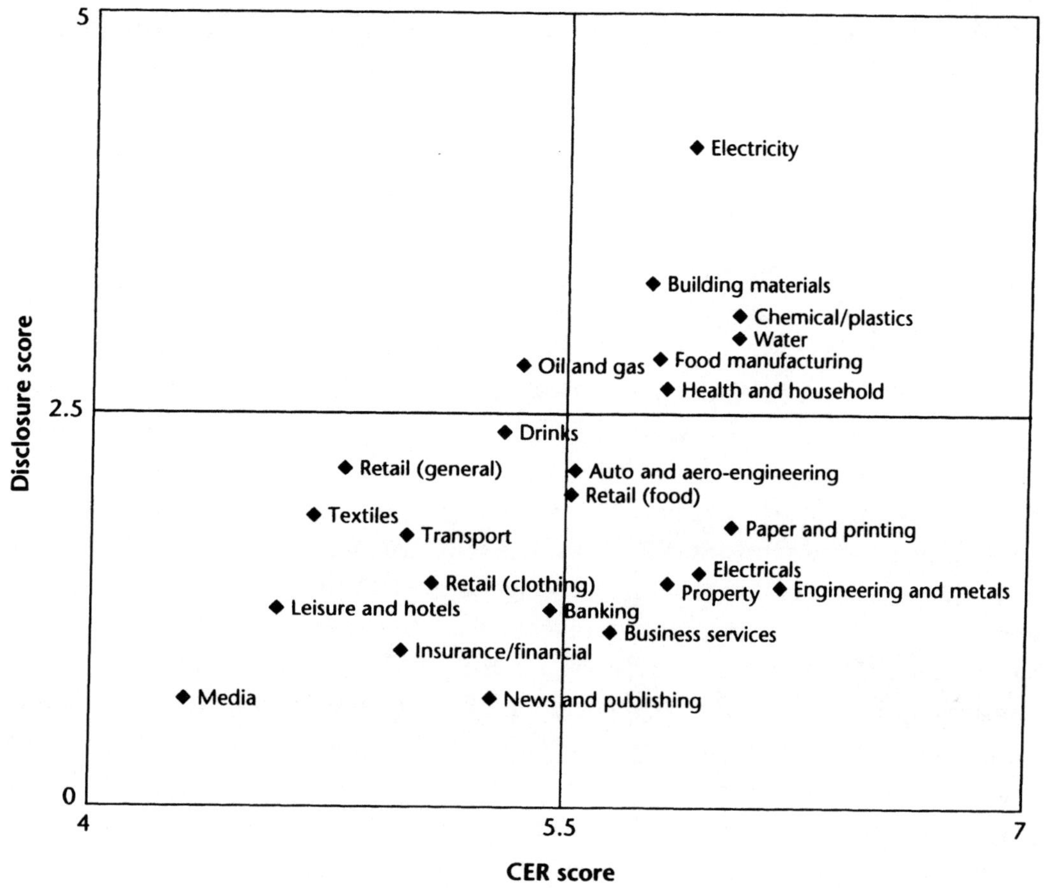

A review of Figure 5.1 suggests an association between CER and disclosure across different industries. In general, the higher the importance of the environment to that industry, the more likely that disclosure will be at a high level. Care is needed in interpreting the CER score, as it does not necessary follow that in non-ES industries executives and analysts award systematically lower scores to their competitors than executives and analysts in ES industries. Clearly, however, those in the top-right quadrant are ES and are consistent with the definitions of ES in previous stages of this research (compare with Figure 4.1). The exception is paper and printing, an industry whose disclosure-quality score was also relatively low compared with other ES industries (Figure 4.5). Recall that the disclosure variable is qualitative, and a score of three or above difficult to imitate by managers not genuinely engaged in environmental activities. For industries in the top-right quadrant, such standards of reporting are the norm for any firm engaged in these activities. Oil and gas would also form part of this standard of environmental management and financial reporting. However, it would appear more difficult for firms in this sector to create convincing environmental reputations. An obvious reason is the impact of high-profile incidents such as the Brent Spar. Shell scored very well before the Brent Spar (seventh, with a score of 6.88), but plummeted in the subsequent survey (146th, with a score of 5.33). The rating system is therefore sensitive to such reputation-destroying incidents. Industries perceived as not directly affected by environmental issues are more likely to be found in the bottom-left quadrant. However, the surprising feature of many is their proximity to the consumer (retailers, drinks and textiles) and therefore their vulnerability to consumer pressure and changing tastes. The disappointing performance of media companies and newspapers is a worrying aspect for those concerned about the environment, in the light of the influence of these organisations on public perceptions. Low priority in their own corporate strategies is likely to be reflected in their methods of promoting the products and activities of other firms. Transport is also in a disappointing position, considering its potential environmental impact as an industry.

It is easy to see why assessors completing the MAC survey may regard banking, insurance and financial as distant from environmental concerns. Beyond paper-recycling initiatives, specific managerial strategies for these industries may be difficult to conceive. However, such a view is potentially superficial. Firms in these industries trade in risk, and risk in turn is likely to be a function of environmental strategies carried out in other firms. In cases like the Brent Spar, it is increasingly likely that insurance firms will pick up the bill. This is not to mention the far broader potential consequences of global warming. Although the relationship is indirect for financial companies, the role of risk is investigated in more detail in the remaining stages of this research. The final quadrant to be considered, the bottom right, shows industries whose position is somewhat equivocal. Engineering and metals, paper and printing, for example, might be considered ES industries, given their relatively high expenditure on environmental protection (Figure 4.1). However, the norms of disclosure in these industries are significantly lower than in other ES industries. Typically, the industries in the top-right quadrant might be subject to a greater degree of regulation compared with those in the bottom right. This may, in part, explain the differences in level of disclosure. An alternative possibility is that these industries have good environmental strategies in place, but these are known only to industry experts and insiders and not signalled to external stakeholders. It may also be the case that hurdle rates for environmental reputation are low for historical reasons, and that there may be first-mover advantages for companies that are able to implement and sustain more specific, monitored, environmental strategies.

5.3.2 *Annual report disclosure and reputation*

Within the constraints of industry benchmarks, there are opportunities for management teams to send quality signals about their environmental policies. Figure 5.2 shows the relationship between the quality of disclosure as defined earlier (Table 3.1) and the CER reputation score. An approximate picture can be obtained from this data about the improvement in reputation that might be generated from a move up the hierarchy of management policy and disclosure. Firms that change from no disclosure at all to the disclosure of at least an outline environmental policy statement can obtain a substantial increase in reputation. As Figure 5.2 suggests, even general rhetoric appears to offer some benefit. If policies are to be stated, it is better to be specific. Generalised environmental policies do not appear to offer any more help than mere rhetoric in creating reputation. Levels 4 and 5 on the disclosure scale offer a further step increase. The implementation and reporting of specific policies and quantifiable targets adds significantly to reputation. Subsequent reporting of actual outcomes against targets (the additional step required to move from 4 to 5 on the scale) has little marginal benefit in terms of reputation.

Figure 5.2 Disclosure quality and environmental reputation

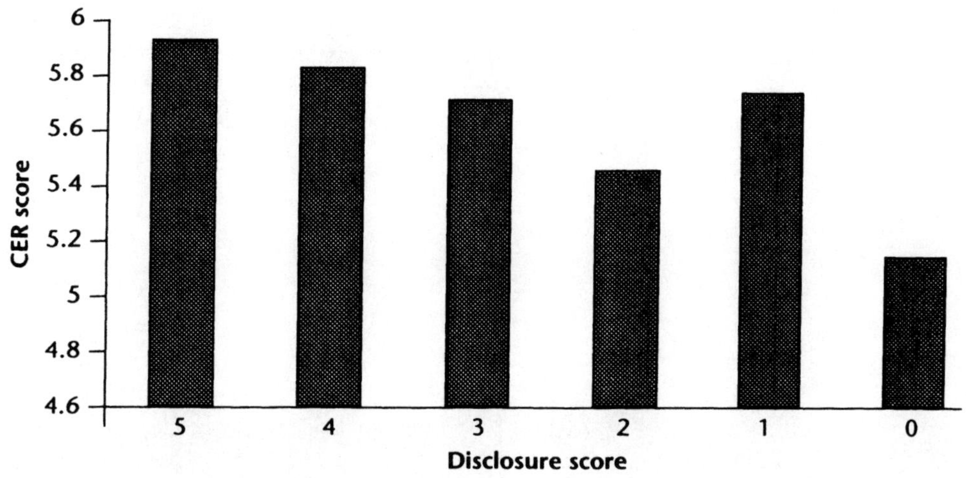

5.3.3 Alternative reputation-building strategies

In addition to direct disclosure in the annual report, there are further strategies open to managers for signalling the quality of their environmental policies. The three investigated here are Kitemark awards, publication of an environmental report and subjecting the firm's procedures to environmental audit. It should be borne in mind that relatively small numbers of companies have Kitemark accreditation in particular (Chapter 3). The numbers using separate environmental reports and environmental auditing were somewhat larger, but tended to be industry specific. The relationship between these three activities and environmental reputation is shown in Figure 5.3. For each strategy considered, companies were grouped 'yes' or 'no' according to published evidence regarding its pursuit (Table 5.2).

Figure 5.3 suggests interesting variations in the impact of environmental strategies and their disclosure on the creation of reputation. As can be observed, achievement and award of Kitemarks does little to enhance environmental reputation. This is consistent with the earlier findings in this survey (Chapter 3) and elsewhere, that Kitemarks have yet to gain credibility and acceptance on a wide scale and have not achieved their objectives of improving environmental management practice (Krut and Gleckman, 1998). The findings also suggest that auditing does not add to reputation. These conclusions are highly tentative, as relatively small numbers of companies are involved and there is significant variation in practice from one industry to another.

In contrast, the publication of a separate environmental report appears to be a particularly effective device. Taking into account the option of issuing an environmental report, there are two disclosure strategies available to management. First, they can issue a comprehensive environmental report and exclude environmental information from the annual report. Alternatively, they can issue substantial quantities of information in both documents. In the latter case, the quality of disclosure on the rating scale used for annual reports above may be lower than it would be otherwise. Examples of companies issuing environmental reports in 1996 and their annual report disclosure scores are shown in Table 5.3.

Figure 5.3 Disclosure strategies as determinants of environmental reputation

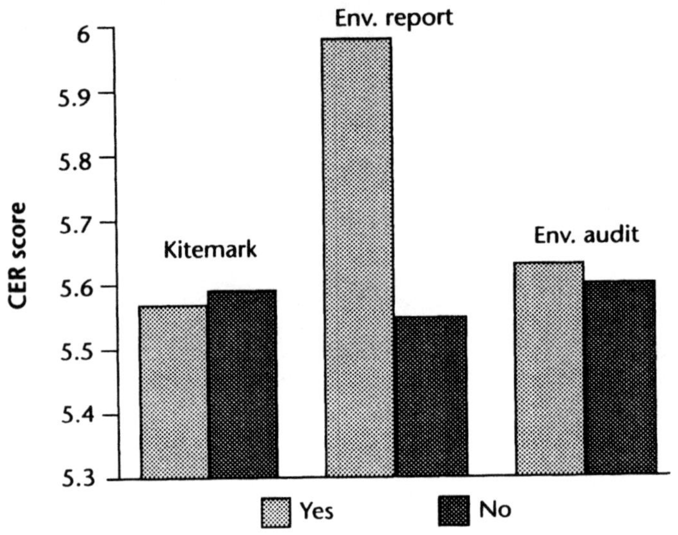

Table 5.3 Sample firms issuing environmental reports in 1996

Company	Disclosure score
Body Shop	4
British Gas	2
British Telecommunications	3
East Midland Electricity	2
English China Clays	3
Glaxo–Wellcome	4
London Electricity	3
National Power	5
P&O	2
Powergen	5
Scottish Power	4
Severn Trent Water	4
Thames Water	4
Thorn–EMI	5
Unilever	4
Wessex Water	3
Yorkshire Electricity	2

In most cases, the companies in Table 5.3 appear to be using both channels of communication simultaneously. In order to examine the relative importance of environmental reporting against the annual report, therefore, further statistical tests were conducted. These tests suggest diminishing economies of scale for environmental reporting beyond the annual report. For example, if environmental management is of good quality and fully consistent to achieve a rating of 5 on the disclosure scale, issuing an environmental report will only have a marginal impact on the environmental reputation of the business. An explanation for the diminished importance of the separate environmental report when evaluated in conjunction with the annual report is that it is seen as merely a spin-off document. It is increasingly common practice for environmental reports to be published and circulated as part of an annual report package. The results here suggest that, in such circumstances, one source of information is sufficient. The study also recognises that there may be other contingencies outside managerial control which may, none the less, influence environmental reputation. These were the presence of block shareholders, firm size, systematic risk, and prior profitability.

5.3.4 Block shareholdings

The impact of the first of these contingencies, block shareholding, is illustrated in Figure 5.4. To more easily present the picture of the effect of block shareholdings, the CER data was grouped into approximately equal quintiles. The quintiles were labelled high to low, with three intermediate levels according to the CER score. As can be seen from Figure 5.4, companies with high reputations for CER tend also to have widely dispersed shareholdings. Following the frameworks discussed in earlier chapters, this is taken to mean that they are therefore held more closely to account by the capital markets.

Figure 5.4 Block shareholding size and environmental reputation

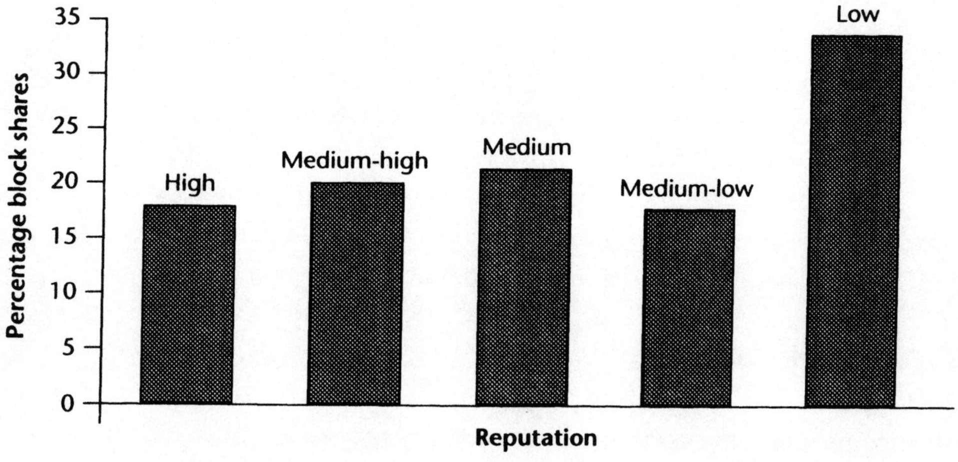

Another significant financial variable is systematic risk. The relationship between environmental reputation and systematic risk measured by beta is illustrated in Figure 5.5. Groupings for environmental reputation are the same as those used in Figure 5.4.

Figure 5.5 Block shareholding size and environmental reputation

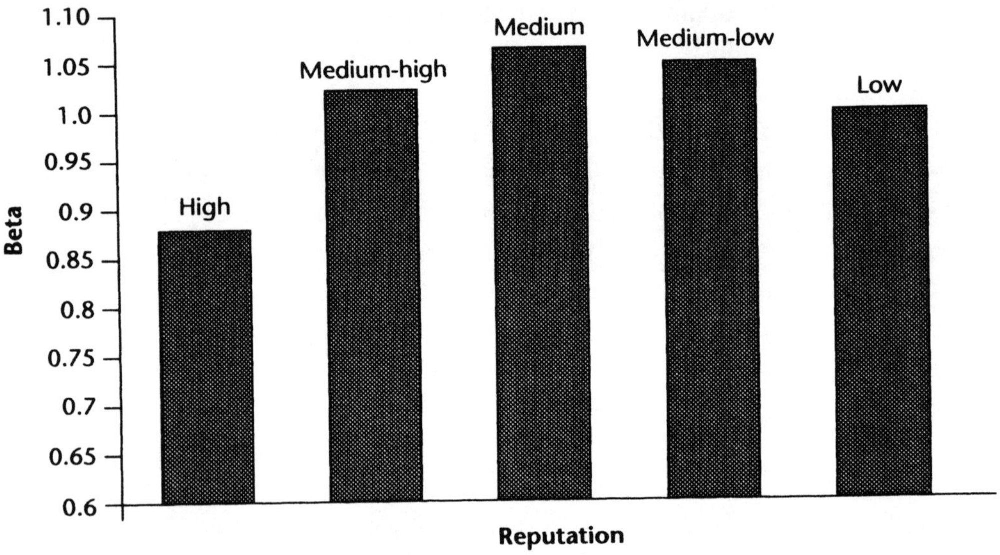

Figure 5.5 shows a broadly negative relationship between systematic risk (BETA) and reputation. In other words, the higher the risk, the more likely a company is to suffer poor environmental reputation. Conversely, there is potentially a real benefit to the creation of environmental reputation since this will tend to lower the cost of capital. Investors holding shares in such companies will require a lower risk-adjusted rate of return. However, the relationship does not appear to hold for companies with very low reputation scores. The main reason is variation between industries. For example, financial companies typically have lower CER scores, possibly because of a perceived irrelevance of environmental issues for their management strategy. However, financial companies have much higher beta factors than non-financials. For example, in the London Business School Risk Measurement Service for January–March 1998, the average beta for financials was 1.28 and for non-financials 0.89. As will be shown in the next chapter, the relationship alters when industry effects are controlled. There are some other caveats to this conclusion. Environmental risk might as easily be specific rather than systematic. There is also the (currently unresolved) controversy over the role of beta in comparing cross-sectional returns. Further research is required, and this issue is explored in more detail in the next chapter.

5.3.5 Prior profitability

Turning to the 'halo' effect, there is no evidence from these results that prior financial performance influences perceptions of environmental reputation. The ROE variable, which averages current performance and the previous two years, was consistently insignificant in all models tested. The same was true of the sales variable that was used to proxy for firm size. However, it would be surprising if no halo was present and, in the light of the US results, further work is required in this area. It is true that there are strong relationships between return on assets, sales, and CER scores in the US research. However, these surveys have used more financial variables than tested above. Although they have relied mainly on accounting data, they have also used stock market value (in book-to-market ratios) as an explanatory variable (Brown and Perry, 1994; Chakravarthy, 1986). None the less, there is a suggestion of some important variations in UK and US conditions. First, there are institutional differences between the UK and the USA, and second, the *Fortune* survey is longer established. It might therefore be expected that the combined effect of these two factors would be to weaken the strength of association between reputation and financial performance in the UK relative to the USA.

5.4 Conclusions

The results suggest that implementation, monitoring and disclosure of environmental policies contribute significantly to the creation of environmental reputation. Diverse share ownership and systematic risk are also associated with environmental reputation. Prior financial performance has no impact, and the halo effect is therefore not supported by the results. The extended stakeholder model is well underpinned by the findings, although the relationship between disclosure and environmental performance is not as predicted by stakeholder models developed in a US context. The association of accounting disclosure and environmental reputation is useful, and will form the basis for further large sample testing of the relationship between green management strategies and competitive advantage, as measured by financial performance differentials.

Key points are that:

- The annual report is the most important form of publicity for creating environmental reputation.
- Reputation is strongly and positively related to the quality of disclosure. Quantification and verifiability will add to reputation more than general policy statements and rhetoric.
- Beyond the annual report, a separate environmental report has a strong effect, but only in circumstances where the same message has not already been signalled via the annual report.
- Environmental auditing and Kitemark accreditation have little effect on reputation, regardless of the annual report disclosure strategy.
- Larger companies with dispersed shareholder bases tend to have higher environmental reputations.
- Firms with higher systematic risk tend to have lower environmental reputations.

6

Environmental Reputation and Profitability

Previous chapters have established relationships between investor perceptions, managerial environmental policies, disclosure of environmental accounting information and the creation of corporate environmental reputation. On the basis of these linkages, this chapter presents a large sample survey of the relationship between corporate environmental responsibility and corporate financial performance. An index of corporate environmental responsibility, which parallels a widely used measure in the USA, is applied to UK companies, whose performances are compared by reference to differentials in accounting and investor appraisal measures.

6.1 Environmental and financial performance: evidence from previous research

A large number of surveys in the United States have been conducted which seek to explain the link between CER and financial performance. The earliest of these found positive associations, although there were diminishing returns to investment in CER after a certain point. This pattern tended to be a feature of surveys relying on monitoring information published by outside regulatory agencies such as US CEP data (Bowman and Haire, 1975; Sturdivant and Ginter, 1977). Other early surveys, using different data, concluded that no significant positive relationship existed (Alexander and Buchholz, 1978; Abbot and Monsen, 1979; Anderson and Frankel, 1980; Freeman and Jaggi, 1982; Cochran and Wood, 1984; Aupperle et al., 1985).

More recently, several studies have concluded that financial performance determines CER. Specifically, these studies have identified the presence of a financial halo effect when using US 'Most Admired Companies' (MAC) data (McGuire et al.,1988; Brown and Perry, 1994). The UK evidence presented in Chapter 5 suggests that the impact of the halo effect may be weaker, although more research is needed here. A final problem in summarising the US research is that it has tended to use differing financial performance measures, and hence it is difficult to discern an overall pattern of relationships.

Perhaps more significantly, there has been no consistent, comprehensive and objective standard for the measurement of CER. An important conclusion in Chapter 5 was the positive association between disclosure strategy and environmental reputation. As has also been pointed out, companies making higher-quality disclosures are more likely to be following genuine and verifiable environmental strategies. Consequently,the MAC ratings have advantages over other methods of assessing environmental performance. For example, some surveys have used measures self-generated by the corporation – for example, accounting disclosures (*inter alia* Bowman and Haire, 1975; Abbot and Monsen, 1979) – without examining the relationship between those disclosures and actual environmental policies. This intermediate step, as conducted in Chapter 5, is important as there is a potential confusion between declared orientation and corporate action (Aupperle et al., 1985; Cochran and Wood, 1984; Arlow and Gannon, 1982; Ullmann, 1985). Other surveys have used measures generated by external agencies – for example, pollution control indices (Spicer, 1978; Chen and Metcalf, 1980). This approach is also potentially biased, for example by dealing with only one particular aspect of CER such as pollution or being likely to reflect opinion without reference to the technical aspects of the particular industry (Bragdon and Marlin, 1972; Cochran and Wood, 1984).

Accordingly, the MAC surveys, based on the responses of objective observers conversant with the industry, offer a way forward as a measure for CER. In the USA, such a survey has been published annually in *Fortune* since 1982. It is based on the views of a large number of managers and investors conversant with the particular industry. The existence of community and environmental responsibility ratings has supported a number of studies in the USA and, as a result, the relationship between environmental performance and financial performance is reasonably well documented (Chakravarthy, 1986; Spencer and Taylor, 1987; McGuire et al., 1988; Herremans et al., 1993). Using UK data, the preceding chapters have to an extent validated the use of MAC ratings. Thus, MAC scores are related to disclosure levels that in turn reflect actual managerial strategies.

The consensus from the US studies would suggest a positive association between environmental and financial performance, notwithstanding the halo effect problem referred to earlier. This may be a function of their common reliance on similar measures, at least as far as environmental performance is concerned. However, there must be limits to the generalisability of these results, which reflect the situation in only one country. Regulatory authorities in the USA since the 1970s have been particularly vigorous in the development of corporate environmental standards and in the enforcement of social and environmental practice disclosure requirements (for example, CEP, 1977). With respect to accounting disclosure, quoted companies are also required to comply with SEC regulations. These include, for example, disclosure of future environmental expenditure (Regulation S-K, Item 101) and the disclosure of potential liabilities arising from environmental problems (SEC Release 6835).

These rules subject large US corporations to a potentially greater degree of scrutiny, and hence litigation, than comparable UK companies. In addition, perceptions of company environmental responsibility are also likely to differ internationally. It is thus considered useful to extend this evidence by reference to and comparison with the performances of UK companies. In doing so, the principal performance measures of previous US surveys are also followed as far as possible. In particular, the UK equivalent of the *Fortune* survey, which has been in commission since 1989, now provides an opportunity to analyse performance over a sufficiently long-run period of time.

6.2 Survey design

A wide range of accounting ratios has been used in the surveys discussed above in order to analyse the relationship between CER and economic performance. Here, the analysis is confined to three. The first hypothesis tests the overall relationship between CER and profitability, as measured by return on capital employed (ROCE), and examines whether there are genuinely superior returns to the strategy of enlightened self-interest.

If this hypothesis is accepted, enlightened self-interest is confirmed as a source of competitive advantage. If investment in environmental responsibility is part of a conscious strategy, it is interesting to observe the components of such policies, and two further hypotheses follow. Creation of corporate image is a useful way to differentiate or to establish market niches. Where such strategies are successful, companies are freed from pressures to undercut competitors and can instead charge higher prices for their apparently unique product. In financial ratio terms, where ROCE is decomposed into its profit margin and asset turnover (AT) elements, differentiation strategies might by expected to result in increases in the former, perhaps at the expense of the latter. Conversely, for a low-cost producer, the opposite might be expected (McNamee, 1988). Thus, if environmental responsibility is part of a corporate or brand image creation strategy, it might be expected that higher prices can be justified to customers. The second hypothesis is therefore that high-CER firms will also have higher profit margins. A third hypothesis follows: that low-CER firms seek competitive advantage through greater production efficiency and faster asset utilisation, and hence will have lower asset turnover ratios. Analysis of return on capital employed and its component ratios will be sufficient to test the extent of relationships between financial performance and managerial decision-making with respect to ethical stance and competitive strategy.

Turning to the view of the stock market investor, if there is an established relationship between CER and return on capital, all rational investors should emulate the ethical investor. However, it might be expected that the ethical investor is also a 'naive' investor, in the sense that a decision is taken not to invest in certain securities regardless of their inclusion in a mean variance efficient portfolio (Simon et al., 1972). These alternative views suggest that the degree of abnormal performance achieved by the investor in firms with good environmental reputation is an empirical question.

To test the existence of superior returns, it is useful to consider the risk-adjusted abnormal return. This is referred to as the Jensen index (Jensen, 1968) and is defined as the difference between the actual return on a share and the risk-adjusted expected return. There are problems associated with using the Jensen measure worth taking into consideration at this stage. It has been shown that returns are systematically related to firm size and book-to-market ratio, although some acknowledge the reasonable scepticism associated with the latter variable (Fama and French, 1996). The test was therefore extended to control for size by using an extended capital asset pricing model approach incorporating a 'size premium', that is, the difference between returns on high and low capitalisation stocks.

For risk measurement, previous surveys have used total risk (standard deviation of return) and systematic risk (the degree of covariance with the market index). The current survey will also use both these measures, plus the residual specific risk. Again, as with the above hypotheses, the relationship between degree of CER and risk will be examined. As far as systematic risk is concerned, it might be postulated that firms which avoid investment in CER are thereby less differentiated and have greater vulnerability to changes in market sentiment. If this were the case, such firms would have higher betas than more responsible firms. Such a view would also be consistent with the results in the previous chapter, and the possibility is examined below. However, important differences might also be expected in the degree of specific risk. For example, it might be expected that risk associated with irresponsibility, such as a chemical spillage, is highly specific to the firm and unconnected with movements in the wider market. Total risk was measured by the variance of return on each security, systematic risk by the beta. Specific risk is taken as the difference between total and systematic risk (for an exact specification of this relationship, see Bodie et al., 1996). As a final comparative, the ratio of abnormal return to specific risk was calculated. This allows us to test the hypothesis that companies with high CER provide investors with access to higher risk-adjusted returns without exposure to increases in specific risk.

ROCE, profit margin and AT data were obtained for sample companies from Datastream. Monthly returns for the period January 1991 to December 1995 were obtained for each sample company and for the FT All-Share Index, and the Treasury Bill Rate from the London Business School Share Price Database. An index of stock market returns for small companies was constructed using the Hoare Govett Small Companies Index (HGSCI), again from the London Business School Share Price Database. CER ratings were obtained from the *Economist* for 1991 and 1992 and from *Management Today* for 1994, 1995, 1996 and 1997 (no survey was conducted for 1993).

It should be borne in mind that accounting rates of return, such as ROCE, and hence profit margin and asset turnover ratios, have the disadvantage of being historically based and being subject to manipulation. Indeed, there has been a considerable debate as to whether they can be relied upon at all. For a summary of these points, see Steele (1995) and Stark (1994) respectively. However, such problems are less relevant in the analysis below, as it is based on a wide cross-section of 22 industries. As accounting returns remain 'the rule of thumb to which decision-makers cling' (Whittington, 1979), these measures seem well justified in the context of the present study. To summarise, the objectives of the tests were to investigate the following:

- In the long run, firms with high CER ratings have significantly higher returns on capital than firms with low CER ratings (where the long run is defined as a five-year period).
- In the long run, firms with higher CER ratings have significantly higher profit margins than firms with low CER ratings.
- In the long run, firms with lower CER have significantly higher AT ratios than firms with higher CER.

- In the long run, firms with higher CER have significantly higher abnormal returns than firms with lower CER.
- In the long run, firms with higher CER have significantly higher systematic, specific and total risk than firms with lower CER.

6.3 Analysis of results

Figure 6.1 shows the relationship between CER and ROCE in the period 1991–7. Average CER scores were calculated for all firms over the period of their individual inclusion in the MAC surveys. Splitting the total sample in two by CER score created subsample groups. The subsample groups were matched by size (measured by sales turnover) and industry. Firms that could not be matched on this basis were discarded. The remaining companies in the two groups were designated 'High CER' and 'Low CER' (Figure 6.1).

Figure 6.1 CER and return on capital

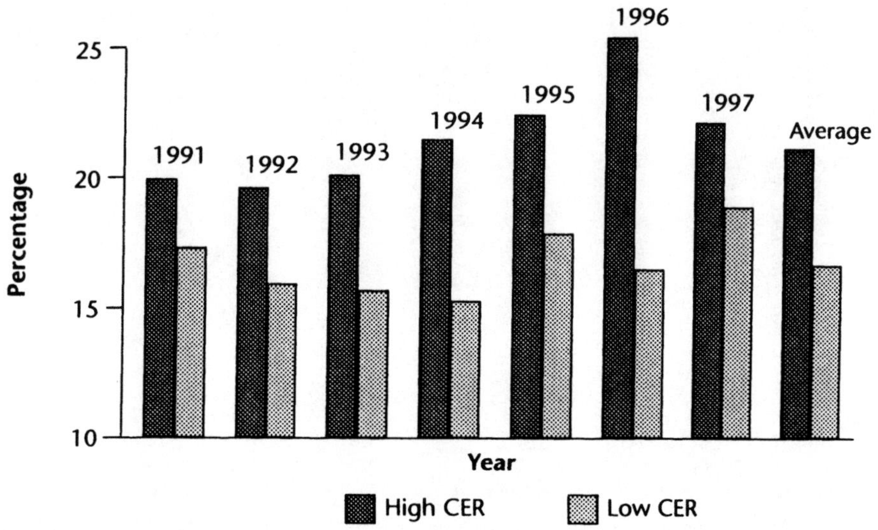

The results shown in Figure 6.1 provide convincing evidence of an association between CER and superior financial performance. An average differential of 4.49 per cent over the seven-year period is strongly significant in statistical terms, with significant differentials at least at the 90 per cent interval being recorded for all years except for 1997. Similar results were obtained when firm size was measured by number of employees instead of sales.

The next step is to analyse these differentials further by examining the subsidiary ratios. Figure 6.2 shows the comparative profit margin ratios of the two subsamples, and Figure 6.3 shows the corresponding asset turnover ratios.

Figure 6.2 CER and profit margin

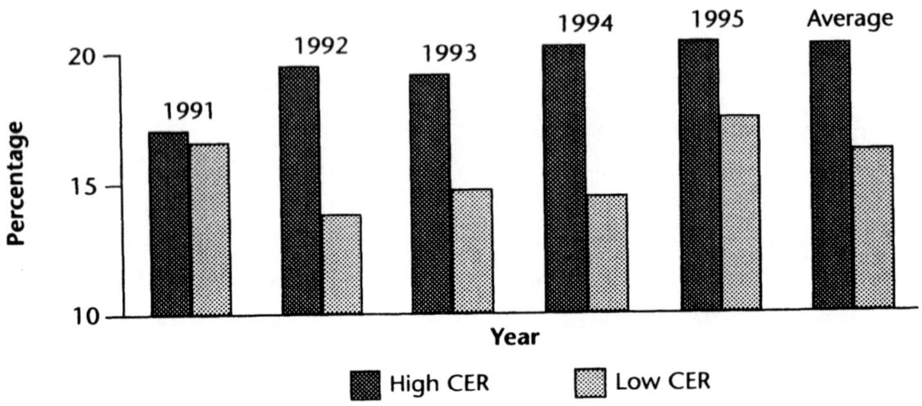

Figure 6.3 CER and asset turnover

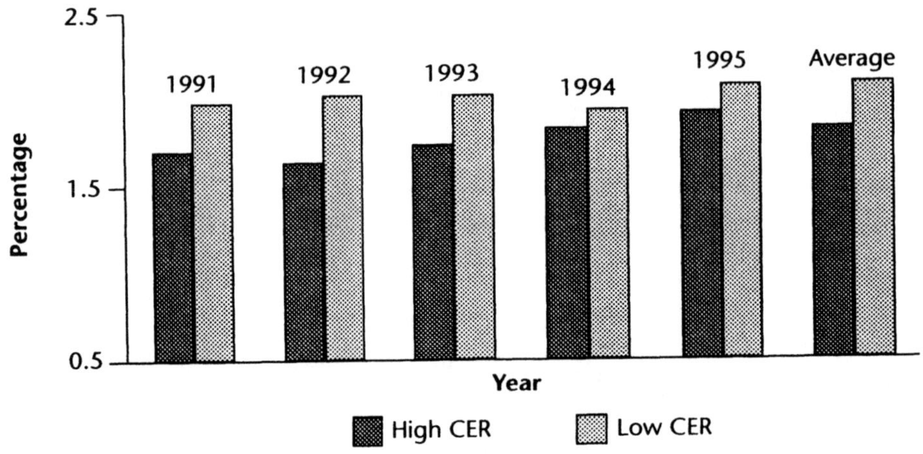

The differentials for the subsidiary ratios are as predicted in the earlier discussion. High-CER companies operate on higher profit margins but lower asset turnover (AT) ratios. Given the likely presence of significant off balance-sheet goodwill assets in this group of companies, the AT might be even lower. There is thus evidence that CER is adopted as an investment in image-building differentiation where the cost is more than recovered through higher prices. Consequently, firms are aware of, and able to exploit, the ethical priorities of consumers. On the other hand, firms which do not invest heavily in CER are able to achieve greater efficiency in asset utilisation, which is perhaps more reflective of their concern with cost. This finding is consistent with other evidence where AT also had a negative sign but was not significant (Cochran and Wood, 1984). The above evidence also needs to be treated with caution. Differentials exist, but they are not consistently significant at high levels of confidence. There are good reasons, arising from the statistical distribution of the ratios, why this should not be the case (Bayldon et al., 1984). Further tests were therefore conducted. First, to reduce the impact of averaging, grouping and loss of sample size in the test above, an ordinary least squares multiple regression, and second, to address the problem of any bias in the subsidiary data, a non-parametric Wilcoxon matched pairs signed rank test. These confirmed the significance of ROCE and also the margin ratio. However, AT remained insignificant in all the models tested. To summarise, in a majority of cases, non-ethically managed companies demonstrate a more efficient use of their assets but only marginally so, and not with any statistical significance. Conversely, ROCE, and to a greater extent margin, are significantly higher for 'ethically' managed firms.

To what extent are these superior accounting returns translated into superior returns for the investor? Comparative abnormal returns for the two subsamples are shown in Figure 6.4. For each subsample, the average risk-adjusted rate of return was computed for the period 1991–5 and the results compared. The comparisons in Figure 6.4 show the abnormal return against stock market benchmarks. The first, alpha, shows the difference between the returns achieved by the subsample group compared with the expected return for the given level of systematic risk. The second, adjusted alpha, shows the difference between the returns achieved by the subsample group compared with the expected return for the given level of systematic risk and the security's market capitalisation.

Figure 6.4 CER and stock market performance

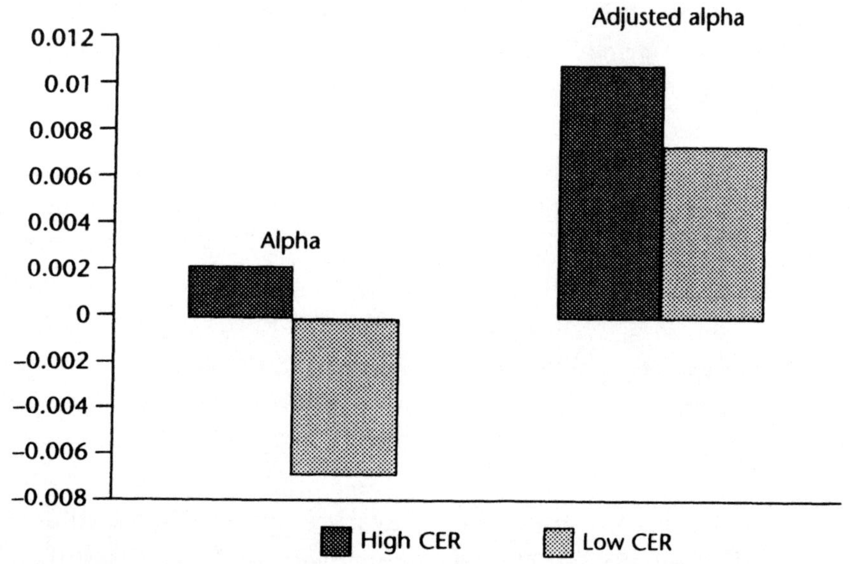

Higher individual security risk-adjusted rates of return in Figure 6.4 are consistent with evidence elsewhere which shows ethical investment funds to have higher, but not conclusively higher, Jensen measures than matched non-ethical funds (Mallin et al., 1995). Such a result is perhaps not surprising, given the superior long-run returns on capital for high-CER companies noted above. It should, none the less, be noted that significance disappears for the adjusted alpha measure, although the hypothesised sign is consistent.

Figure 6.5 CER and stock market risk

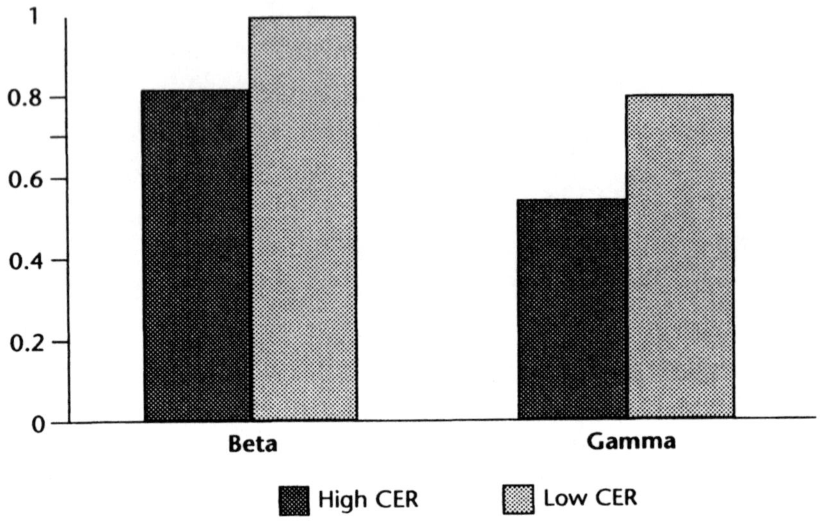

Figure 6.5 compares the risk attributes of the subsamples. Each is compared with reference to systematic risk (beta) and exposure to systematic differences in returns on the smaller companies index (gamma). Comparing the risk attributes that are shown in Figure 6.5, betas and gammas were significantly lower for the ethical companies. Note that, in Chapter 5, there was a less clear-cut relationship between beta and CER. In this case, however, the betas are compared over a longer period (five years) and on the basis of matched samples controlling for size and industry. Such evidence is consistent with the hypothesis of lower variability in underlying returns. The standard deviation of ROCE for high-CER companies was 17.5 per cent compared with 28.1 per cent for low-CER companies. Considering beta alone in the context of arriving at a cost of capital in capital budgeting, there is a suggestion of lower hurdle rates for higher-CER companies. Many companies use beta in calculations of this description. Assuming they use a long-run average risk premium of 8 per cent, the difference in simple betas of 0.169 would translate into a lower cost of equity capital of approximately 1.35 per cent. When the betas were recalculated controlling for the effect of gamma (Figure 6.5) the differential in favour of high-CER companies was slightly higher (0.183, leading to a reduction of 1.5 per cent in the cost of equity capital).

In contrast, comparative total risk as measured by the standard deviation of market returns for the two subsamples had only a very small and insignificant difference (0.00640 for high-CER compared with 0.00777 for low-CER). While systematic risk and total risk were higher for the non-ethical group, companies with high responsibility ratings had slightly higher specific risk, although the difference was not significant. When abnormal returns and specific risk are combined in the appraisal ratio, the high-CER group demonstrates a highly significant difference (0.21597 for high-CER compared with –1.2165 for low-CER). To summarise, high-CER companies provide access to abnormal returns but without a corresponding jump in total risk, and with significantly lower systematic risk.

Such securities are therefore likely to be sought after by the investment analyst seeking higher reward-to-volatility trade-offs. An investor seeking abnormal returns can do so by selecting from high-CER companies while not incurring a proportionate increase in risk. Risk-adjusted out-performance at individual company level appears to be better supported on the basis of this evidence than comparable results for investment funds (compare Mallin et al., 1995). In other surveys, weak evidence of over-performance by ethical unit trusts has been attributed to a tendency of such funds to invest in smaller companies (Luther et al., 1992; Gregory, et al., 1997). Note, however, the result in Chapter 2 which suggested that ethical fund managers expect larger companies to have higher CER. Although size effects are also important, the evidence from the above tests points to a further possible reason: that ethical funds may be insufficiently discriminatory in their stock selection. For example, a typical fund may simply avoid certain industries, such as alcohol, defence, tobacco, etc. The current survey, in contrast, has matched examples of good/bad practice within many industries that an ethical fund might ignore completely. What is also likely, and to be expected given the generality, incompleteness and propagandist nature of much social and environmental reporting, is that market analysts do not fully incorporate measures of CER (Harte and Owen, 1991, and Chapter 2 above).

6.4 Conclusions

The evidence presented above suggests that there is a strong association between CER and superior economic performance. This relationship for UK companies supports the consensus view emerging from many years of similar research in the USA, although further work needs to be done in both countries on the direction of causality. It should be noted, however, that the lagged profit variable discussed in Chapter 5 did not perform as well as the contemporaneous measures used in this chapter. UK evidence, much of which is analysed above for the first time, suggests that consensus might be transferable internationally, notwithstanding regulatory and cultural differences between the UK and the USA.

Superior profits for high-CER companies are driven by marketing rather than productive efficiency. Crucially, the required sacrifice in efficient asset utilisation is disproportionately small *vis-à-vis* the likely gains from improved margins. Increasingly, therefore, companies might be prepared to sacrifice efficient usage of their assets to more than recover investment in image through higher margins. 'Greenness', and other forms of environmental responsibility, are essentially marketing weapons.

The ability of firms to exploit such strategies would appear to provide opportunities for the investor. Although not conclusive, superior risk-adjusted returns on individual securities should also in theory translate into superior returns for ethical investment funds, although to achieve accounting profitability superior returns stock selection methods might require analysis of good CER practice in industries usually regarded as 'unethical'.

Key points are that:

- Higher-CER companies have an average accounting profitability premium of approximately 4.5 per cent.
- Higher-CER companies have an average stock market risk-adjusted return premium of approximately 0.89 per cent.
- The premium is driven by superior profit margins.
- Higher-CER companies have lower average betas. As a result, their cost of equity capital is lower by approximately 1.35 per cent.

7

Conclusions

The research project has examined the extent to which companies can prosper financially while paying attention to the environment as an important stakeholder. This may be a defining issue for businesses in the twenty-first century. For the accountant, it raises concerns about the fundamentals of financial reporting. These include those that have been addressed in this project. What information do the providers of finance to businesses require (Chapter 2)? How should that information be disclosed and communicated (Chapters 3 and 4)? How does the provision of such information assist management in building a reputation for good environmental practice (Chapter 5)? Is that reputation thus created associated with superior financial returns (Chapter 6)? At the end of each chapter a list of key points was provided, and these are reproduced here.

Chapter 2 key points

Companies that follow the environmental policies listed below are likely to enjoy better reputations for environmental responsibility in investment institutions. To secure this reputation, management should consider the following:

- Engage in environmental expenditure beyond the requirements of current legislation and in anticipation of future legislation.
- Ensure that such expenditure is properly appraised.
- Make effective use of the annual report to add credibility to environmental management strategies. Publish quantified, auditable targets where possible and use them as benchmarks for actual performance.
- Support the annual report themes with presentations to investors.

Chapter 3 key points

- In the very near future the inclusion of environmental information of some kind will be expected as standard for most large UK plcs.
- The quality of environmental disclosure is increasing.
- The annual report is a more widely used and strategic means of communication than a separate environmental report.
- Environmental auditing is not commonplace and is probably below the expectation level of the investment community.
- Very few firms have responded to the opportunities offered by Kitemark schemes.

Chapter 4 key points

- Non-family-owned firms with dispersed share ownership have higher-quality environmental disclosures.
- Larger firms have higher-quality environmental disclosures.
- Capital expenditure on environmental projects is associated with higher-quality disclosure in environmentally sensitive industries. Industry norms and voluntary codes of practice may also drive such disclosures.
- Environmental disclosure does not increase in response to greater use of debt finance or higher systematic risk.
- Environmental disclosure does not increase in response to *ex ante* profitability and hence cash flow.

Chapter 5 key points

- The annual report is the most important form of publicity for creating environmental reputation.
- Reputation is strongly and positively related to the quality of disclosure. Quantification and verifiability will add to reputation more than general policy statements and rhetoric.
- Beyond the annual report, a separate environmental report has a strong effect, but only in circumstances where the same message has not already been signalled via the annual report.
- Environmental auditing and Kitemark accreditation have little effect on reputation regardless of the annual report disclosure strategy.
- Larger companies with dispersed shareholder bases tend to have higher environmental reputations.
- Firms with higher systematic risk tend to have lower environmental reputations.

Chapter 6 key points

- Higher-CER companies have an average accounting profitability premium of approximately 4.5 per cent.
- Higher-CER companies have an average stock market risk-adjusted return premium of approximately 0.89 per cent.
- The premium is driven by superior profit margins.
- Higher-CER companies have lower average betas. As a result, their cost of equity capital is lower by approximately 1.35 per cent.

It is hoped that, in the light of the theoretical framework of Chapter 1, the consistency of the results throughout the empirical surveys, and the relatively large samples used, some confidence can be placed in the financial premium suggested in Chapter 6. If so, a consequence of this research may be greater voluntary adoption of environmental management techniques. Indeed, against a background of growing international consensus, it is perhaps important that both accountants and investors recognise the premium available to CER, the former by establishing appropriate conduits of accountability, the latter rewarding good behaviour through investment decision-making. As for economists, there might be an encouragement to move away from single stakeholder analytical models. Lastly, while it is unlikely that regulation can be ruled out, the promise of better financial returns could be a useful argument for regulatory agencies faced with the need to persuade reluctant corporations to take greater account of the wider stakeholder community.

This research does not propose any solutions to the problems of environmental degradation. That would remain the case even if companies were to adopt the suggested systems of environmental disclosure that are truthful, verifiable, and favourably impress risk-averse return-maximising investors. As Hawkin puts it, 'if every company on the planet were to adopt the social and environmental practices of the best companies – of, say, the Body Shop ... – the world would still be moving towards environmental degradation and collapse' (cited in Pearce and Tombs, 1998). Under conditions of high capital mobility, globalisation may lead enough firms to avoid regulatory pressures through international diversification. Ethical behaviour towards the environment by individual companies will not reverse global processes overnight. None the less, as the research has shown, it does offer the prospect of competitive advantage to progressive companies. That may at least be a start.

Bibliography

Abbott, W.F. and Monsen, R.J. (1979), 'On the Measurement of Corporate Social Responsibility: Self-Reported Disclosures as a Method of Measuring Corporate Social Involvement', *Academy of Management Journal*, 22, 3, pp. 501–15.

Adams, R. (1998), 'Publications', *Environmental Accounting and Auditing Reporter*, vol. 3 (8).

Alexander, G. and Buchholz, A. (1978), 'Corporate Social Responsibility and Stock Market Performance', *Academy of Management Journal*, vol. 21 (3), pp. 479–86.

Anderson, J.C. and Frankel, A.W. (1980), 'Voluntary Social Reporting: An Isobeta Portfolio Analysis', *Accounting Review*, vol. 55, pp. 467–79.

Arlow, P. and Gannon, M. (1982), 'Social Responsiveness, Corporate Structure, and Economic Performance', *Academy of Management Review*, vol. 7, pp. 235–6.

Aupperle, K.E., Carroll, A. and Hatfield, J. (1985), 'An Empirical Examination of the Relationship between Corporate Social Responsibility and Profitability', *Academy of Management Journal*, vol. 28 (2), pp. 446–63.

Barker, V. and Duhaime, I. (1997), 'Strategic Change in the Turnaround Process: Theory and Empirical Evidence', *Strategic Management Journal*, vol. 18 (1), pp. 13–38.

Barney, J.B. (1991), 'Firm Resources and Sustained Competitive Advantage', *Journal of Management*, vol. 17, pp. 99–120.

Barton, S., Hill, N. and Sudasaram, S. (1989), 'An Empirical Test of Stakeholder Predictions of Capital Structure', *Financial Management*, Spring, pp. 36–44.

Bayldon, R., Woods, A. and Zafiris, N. (1984), 'A Note on the "Pyramid" Technique of Financial Ratio Analysis of Firms' Performance', *Journal of Business Finance and Accounting*, vol. 11 (1), pp. 99–106.

Belkaoui, A. (1984), *Socio-Economic Accounting*, Connecticut: Quorum.

Benjamin, J.J. and Stanga, K.G. (1977), 'Difference in Disclosure Needs of Major Users of Financial Statements', *Accounting and Business Research*, vol. 27, Summer, pp. 187–92.

Bodie, Z., Kane, A. and Marcus, A. (1996), *Investments*, Chicago: Irwin (3rd Edition).

Bowman, E.H. and Haire, M. (1975), 'A Strategic Posture Toward Corporate Social Responsibility', *California Management Review*, XVIII, 2, pp. 49–58.

Bradley, I.C. (1987), *Enlightened Entrepreneurs*, London: Weidenfeld and Nicolson.

Bragdon, J. and Marlin, J.A.T. (1972), 'Is Pollution Profitable? Environmental Virtue and Reward: Must Stiffer Polution Controls Hurt Profits?', *Risk Management*, April, pp. 9–18.

Brown, B. and Perry, S. (1994), 'Removing the Financial Performance Halo from *Fortune*'s "Most Admired" Companies', *Academy of Management Journal*, vol. 37 (5), pp. 1347–59.

Cannon, T. (1994), *Corporate Responsibility,* London: Pitman.

Caporaso, J. and Levine, D. (1992), *Theories of Political Economy,* Cambridge: Cambridge University Press.

CEP (1997), *The Pollution Audit: A Guide to 50 Industrials for Responsible Investors.* CEP.

Chakravarthy, B. (1986), 'Measuring Strategic Performance', *Strategic Management Journal,* vol. 7, pp. 437–58.

Chen, K.H. and Metcalf, R.W. (1980), 'The Relationship between Pollution Control Record and Financial Indicators Revisited', *Accounting Review;* vol. 55 (1), pp. 168–77.

Chenall, R.H. and Juchau, R. (1977), 'Investor Information Needs: An Australian Study', *Accounting and Business Research,* vol. 26, Spring, pp. 111–19.

Cochran, P.L. and Wood R.A. (1984), 'Corporate Social Responsibility and Financial Performance', *Academy of Management Journal,* vol. 27 (1), pp. 42–56.

Copeland, T.E., Koller, T. and Murrin, J. (1994), *Valuation: Measuring and Managing the Value of Companies,* New York Wiley.

Cowen, S., Ferreri, L. and Parker, L. (1987), 'The Impact of Corporate Characteristics on Social Responsibility Disclosure: Typology and Frequency-based Results', *Accounting, Organizations and Society,* vol. 12, pp. 111–22.

Department of the Environment (1996), Environmental Protection Expenditure by Industry, London: HSMO.

Dierkes, M. and Preston, L. (1977), 'Corporate Social Accounting Reporting for the Physical Environment: A Critical Review and Implementation Proposal,' *Accounting, Organizations and Society,* vol. 2 (1), pp. 3–22.

Dierkes, M. and Antal, A.B. (1985), 'Corporate Social Reporting in Germany: Conceptual Developments and Practical Experience', *Accounting, Organizations and Society,* vol. 4, no. 1/2, pp. 87–107.

Donaldson, T. and Preston, L.E. (1995), 'The Stakeholder Theory of the Corporation: Concepts, Evidence, and Implications', *Academy of Management Review,* 20, 1, pp. 65–91.

Dye, R. (1986), 'Disclosure of Nonproprietary Information', *Journal of Business,* vol. 59, no. 1, pp. 331–66.

Fama, E.F. and French, K.R. (1996), 'Multifactor Explanations of Asset Pricing Anomalies', *Journal of Finance,* vol. 51, no. 1, pp. 55–84.

Firth, M. (1979), 'The Impact of Size, Stockmarket Listing and Auditors on Voluntary Disclosure in Corporate Annual Reports', *Accounting and Business Research,* Autumn, pp. 273–80.

Firth, M. (1984), 'The Extent of Voluntary Disclosure in Annual Reports and its Association with Risk Measures', *Applied Economics,* vol. 16, pp. 269–77.

Fombrun, C. and Shanley, M. (1990), 'What's in a Name? Reputation Building and Corporate Strategy', *Academy of Management Journal,* vol. 33, pp. 233–56.

Frederick, W.C., Davis, K. and Post, J.E. (1988), *Business and Society: Corporate Strategy, Public Policy, Ethics,* New York: McGraw-Hill.

Freeman, M. and Jaggi, B. (1982), 'An Analysis of the Impact of Corporate Pollution

Disclosures Included in Annual Financial Statements on Investment Decisions', *Advances in Public Interest Accounting,* vol. 1, pp. 193–212.

Friedman, M. (1962), *Capitalism and Freedom,* Chicago: University of Chicago Press.

Friedman, M. (1970), 'A Friedman Doctrine: The Social Responsibility of Business is to Increase its Profits' *New York Times Magazine,* pp. 32–3,123–5.

Fry, F. and Hock, R. (1976), 'Who Claims Corporate Social Responsibility? The Biggest and the Worst', *Business and Society Review,* vol. 18, pp. 62–5.

Fryxell, C. and Wang, J. (1994), 'The *Fortune* Corporate "Reputation" Index: Reputation for What?', *Journal of Management,* vol. 20 (1), pp. 1–14.

Gibbins, M., Richardson, A. and Waterhouse, J. (1990), 'The Management of Corporate Financial Disclosure: Opportunism, Ritualism, Policies and Process', *Journal of Accounting Research,* vol. 28 (Spring), pp. 121–43.

Gray, R., Kouhy, R. and Lavers, S. (1995), 'Corporate Social and Environmental Reporting: A Review of the Literature and a Longitudinal Study of UK Disclosure, *Accounting, Auditing and Accountability Journal,* 8, 2, pp. 47–77.

Gregory, A., Matatko, J. and Luther, R. (1997), 'Ethical Unit Trust Financial Performance: Small Company Effects and Fund Size Effects', *Journal of Business Finance and Accounting,* vol. 24, no. 5, pp. 705–25.

Guthrie, J. and Parker, L.D. (1989), 'Corporate Social Reporting: A Rebuttal of Legitimacy Theory', *Accounting and Business Research,* vol. 9, no. 76, pp. 343–52.

Guthrie, J. and Parker, L.D. (1990), 'Corporate Social Disclosure Practice: A Comparative International Perspective', *Advances in Public Interest Accounting,* vol. 4, pp. 159–75.

Hall, R. (1992), 'The Strategic Analysis of Intangible Resources', *Strategic Management Journal,* vol. 13, pp. 135–44.

Harte, G., Lewis, L. and Owen, D. (1991), 'Ethical Investment and the Corporate Reporting Function', *Critical Perspectives on Accounting,* vol. 2, no. 3, pp. 123–42.

Harte, G. and Owen, D. (1991), 'Environmental Disclosure in the Annual Reports of British Companies: A Research Note', *Accounting, Auditing and Accountability Journal,* vol. 4, pp. 51–61.

Harte, G. and Owen, D. (1992), 'Current Trends in the Reporting of Green Issues in the Annual Reports of UK Companies', in Owen, D. (ed.), *Green Reporting – Accounting and the Challenge of the Nineties,* London: Chapman & Hall.

Herremans, I.M., Akathaporn, P. and McInnes, M. (1993), 'An Investigation of Corporate Social Responsibility Reputation and Economic Performance', *Accounting, Organizations and Society,* vol. 18 (7/8), pp. 587–604.

Heyes, A.G. (1998), 'Making Things Stick: Enforcement and Compliance', *Oxford Review of Economic Policy,* vol. 14, no. 4, pp. 50–62.

Howes, R., Skea, J. and Whelan, B. (1997), *Clean and Competitive: Motivating Environmental Performance in Industry,* London: Earthscan.

Ingram, R.W. (1978), 'An Investigation of the Information Content of (Certain) Social Responsibility Disclosures', *Journal of Accounting Research,* 16, 2, pp. 270–85.

Jensen, M. (1968), 'The Performance of Mutual Funds in the Period 1945–1964',

Journal of Finance, vol. XXIII (2), pp. 389–415.

Jensen, M. (1986), 'The Agency Costs of Free Cash Flow: Corporate Finance and Takeovers', *American Economic Review,* vol. 76, pp. 323–9.

Jensen, M. and Meckling, W. (1976), 'Theory of the Firm: Managerial Behaviour, Agency Costs and Capital Structure', *Journal of Financial Economics,* vol. 3, pp. 305–60.

Jones, S., Romano, C.A. and Smyrnios K.X. (1995), 'An Evaluation of the Decision Usefulness of Cash Flow Statements by Australian Reporting Entities', *Accounting and Business Research,* vol. 25, no. 98, pp.115–29.

Keim, G. (1978), 'Corporate Social Responsibility: An Assessment of the Enlightened Self-Interest Model', *Academy of Management Review,* January, pp. 32–9.

Krut, R. and Gleckman, H. (1998), *ISO14001: A Missed Opportunity for Global Industrial Development,* London: Earthscan.

Levitt, T. (1970), 'The Dangers of Social Responsibility', *Harvard Business Review,* July/August.

Luther, R., Matako, J. and Corner, D. (1992), 'The Investment Performance of UK "Ethical" Unit Trusts', *Accounting, Auditing and Accountability Journal,* vol. 5 (4), pp. 57–70.

Macve, R. and Carey, A. (eds) (1992), B*usiness, Accountancy and the Environment: A Policy and Research Agenda,* London: ICAEW.

Mahapatra, S. (1984), 'Investor Reaction to Corporate Social Accounting', *Journal of Business Finance and Accounting,* vol. 11 (1), pp. 29–40.

Mallin, C., Saadouni, B. and Briston, R. (1995), 'The Financial Performance of Ethical Investment Funds', *Journal of Business Finance and Accounting,* 22 (4), pp. 483–96.

McGuire, J., Schneeweis, T. and Branch, B. (1990), 'Perceptions of Firm Quality: A Cause or Result of Firm Performance', *Journal of Management,* vol. 16 (1), pp. 167–80.

McGuire, J., Sundgren, A. and Schneeweis, T. (1988), 'Corporate Social Responsibility and Firm Financial Performance', *Academy of Management Journal,* vol. 31 (4), pp. 854–72.

McNamee, K. (1988), *Tools and Techniques of Strategic Management,* Oxford: Pergamon.

Moskowitz, M.R. (1972), 'Choosing Socially Responsible Stock', *Business and Society Review,* vol. 1, pp. 71–5.

Neu, D., Warsame, H. and Pedwell, K. (1998), 'Managing Public Impressions: Environmental Disclosures in Annual Reports', *Accounting, Organizations and Society,* 23, 3, pp. 265–82.

Patten, D. (1991), 'Exposure, Legitimacy, and Social Disclosure', *Journal of Accounting and Public Policy,* vol. 10, pp. 297–308.

Patten, D. (1992), 'Intra-industry Environmental Disclosures in Response to the Alaskan Oil Spill: A Note on Legitimacy Theory', *Accounting, Organizations and Society,* 17, 5, pp. 471–5.

Pearce, F. and Tombs, S. (1998), *Toxic Capitalism: Corporate Crime and the Chemical Industry,* Aldershot: Ashgate.

Perks, R., Rawlinson, D. and Ingram, L. (1992), 'An Exploration of Ethical Investment in the UK', *British Accounting Review,* vol. 24 (1), pp. 43–66.

Porter, M.E. (1985), *Competitive Advantage,* New York: Free Press.

Porter, M.E. and Van der Linde, C. (1996), 'Green and Competitive: Ending the Stalemate', in Welford,

Preston, L. (1978), 'Analysing Corporate Social Performance: Methods and Results', *Journal of Contemporary Business,* vol. 7, pp. 135–50.

Roberts, R.W. (1992), 'Determinants of Corporate Social Responsibility Disclosure: An Application of Stakeholder Theory', *Accounting, Organizations and Society,* 17, 6, pp. 595–612.

Robertson, D. and Nicholson, N. (1996), 'Expressions of Corporate Responsibility in UK Firms', *Journal of Business Ethics,* vol. 15 (10), pp. 1095–106.

Rockness, J. (1985), 'An Assessment of the Relationship between US Corporate Environmental Performance and Disclosure', *Journal of Business Finance and Accounting,* vol. 12, pp. 339–54.

Rockness, J. and Williams, P.F. (1988), 'A Descriptive Study of Social Responsibility Mutual Funds', *Accounting, Organizations and Society,* 13, 4, pp. 397–411.

Simon, J., Powers, C. and Gunneman, J. (1972), *The Ethical Investor,* New Haven, Conn.: Yale University Press.

Spence, A. (1973), 'Job Market Signalling', *Quarterly Journal of Economics,* vol. 87, pp. 355–79.

Spencer, B.A. and Taylor, G.S. (1987), 'A Within and Between Analysis of the Relationship between Corporate Social Responsibility and Financial Performance', *Akron Business and Economic Review,* vol. 18 (3), pp. 7–18.

Spicer, B. (1978), 'Investors, Corporate Social Performance and Information Disclosure: An Empirical Study', *Accounting Review,* LIII, 1, pp. 94–111.

Stark, A. (1994), 'Some Analytics of why Conditional IRRs can contain Growth-related Measurement Error', *Journal of Business Finance and Accounting,* vol. 21, no. 2, pp. 219–30.

Steele, A. (1995), 'Further Notes on Estimating Economic Returns from Published Accounting Statements', *Journal of Business Finance and Accounting,* vol. 22, no. 7, pp. 923–38.

Sturdivant, F.D. and Ginter, J.L. (1977), 'Corporate Social Responsiveness', *California Management Review,* vol. 19 (3), pp. 30–9.

Tinker, T. (1991), 'The Accountant as Partisan', *Accounting, Organizations and Society,* vol. 16, pp. 297–310.

Tonkin, D. and Skerrett, L.C.L (1991), *Financial Reporting, 1990–1: A Survey of UK Reporting Practice,* London: ICAEW.

Trotman, K.T. and Bradley, G.W. (1981), 'Associations between Social Responsibility Disclosure and Characteristics of Companies', *Accounting, Organizations and Society,* vol. 6, pp. 355–62.

Ullmann, A.A. (1985), 'Data in Search of a Theory: A Critical Examination of the Relationships among Social Performance, Social Disclosure and Economic Performance of US Firms', *Academy of Management Review,* 10, 3, pp. 540–57.

United Nations Environment Programme (1994), *Company Environmental Reporting: A Measure of the Progress of Business and Industry Towards Sustainable Development*, Technical Report 24, Paris: UNEP.

Wagner, G. (1987), *The Chocolate Conscience*, London: Chatto and Windus.

Watts, R. and Zimmerman, J. (1986), *Positive Accounting Theory*, Englewood Cliffs, NJ: Prentice Hall.

Whittington, G. (1979), 'On the Use of the Accounting Rate of Return in Empirical Research', *Accounting and Business Research*, vol. 9, no. 35, pp. 201–8.

Wiseman, J. (1982), 'An Evaluation of Environmental Disclosures made in Corporate Annual Reports', *Accounting, Organizations and Society*, vol. 7, pp. 53–63.

Yap, C. (1997), 'Users' Perceptions of the Need for Cash Flow Statements – Australian Evidence', *European Accounting Review*, vol. 6, no. 4, pp. 653–72.

Zadek, S., Pruzan, P. and Evans, R. (1997), *Building Corporate Accountability*, London: Earthscan.

Printed in the United States
86685LV00002B

The Chartered Institute of Management Accountants
63 Portland Place, London W1N 4AB
Telephone: +44 (0)20 7917 9277 Fax: +44 (0)20 7323 1487